* * *

Trading Course

Trading Course

How to Become a Consistently Winning Trader

Henrique M. Simões

ISBN: 1540433803
ISBN-13: 9781540433800
Library of Congress Control Number: 2016919278
CreateSpace Independent Publishing Platform
North Charleston, South Carolina

To Enzo

Contents

Chapter 1

First Things First

Welcome to the trading course that could change your life. I'm Henrique, the author of this trading course and a professional futures trader. I have been actively trading the markets since 1999, but I needed thousands of trades and years of experience to become a successful trader. Most traders get lost in the process and give up trading before they achieve the necessary level of expertise to win in the markets consistently, but I have designed this course to be your shortcut to successful trading—a way for you to discover what is really important for your trading success by shortening the trial-and-error period every trader has to go through before being successful.

1.1 Your Final Goal

A very successful trader once said there is always a way to make money, regardless of market or time frame. As a trader, your job is to find it. This structured course has that end in mind and will help you become a consistent, winning trader with a distinctive trading signature. These are your final goals for this course.

Before we start exploring topics this course will cover, I would like to outline a few important concepts you should take away from your reading.

Most People Make a Big Deal out of Market Prediction

The most successful traders do not predict markets—they leave that for financial commentators, economists, and analysts. Consistently winning traders follow the signals generated by their systems, strategies, or methodologies. They get out when their stops are hit or their trading edge is no longer present or active. They do not take profits before their methods tell them to. Successful traders also look for many opportunities to exploit their trading edge; this makes them less likely to experience losing months in their accounts. Most traders do not understand this line of thought. As a result, they try to predict the market direction and fail to achieve the desired trading consistency.

Why are so few people able to make money trading the markets? My answer is that profitable trading requires both technical and psychological skills—even if you have a good technical knowledge of the markets, this is not enough per se to make you a consistently winning trader. We will discuss this in depth throughout the course. In the meantime, remember that an investment in knowledge pays the best interest.

Homework: *Why I am taking this course?* Think of a few reasons and write them down.

(Homework questions will appear throughout the course. Answer these as thoroughly you can. Grab a pencil, an eraser, and a piece of paper, and write and rewrite until you feel you've answered them completely.)

1.2 Who Should Take This Course

Traders in all stages of development will benefit from this course. In trading, the equity curve is the perfect reflection of your actual trading strengths and weaknesses, which means you are only as good as the shape of your equity curve. That is your starting point. All the improvements you make going forward should be reflected in the future shape of your equity curve. Ideally, your equity curve should stretch from the lower left to the upper right and should be as steep and as smooth as possible.

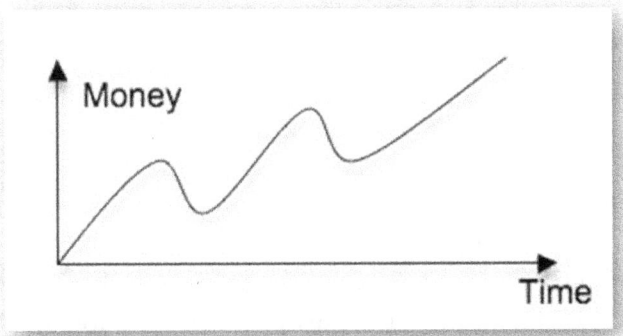

This also means you need to acknowledge and accept that you—and not the market—are completely responsible for your success or failure as a trader.

Homework: Plot your equity curve for the last year or two. Make a critical assessment of your current stage of development as a trader.

1.3 The Necessary Commitment

The most successful traders do not think twice about how many hours they have to spend at their desks or whether they have to do some extra research on a weekend. That is commitment.

Over a recent weekend, I had to backtest two trading strategies to decide which provided the better outcome. If you want to perform at a very high level as a trader, you can't have any doubts in your mind and need to have confidence in your trading strategies. From time to time, this means you need to make an extra effort, just to stay ahead of your competitors and on top of your own game.

It's quite a long journey to become a consistent winner trading the markets, and that is, in my opinion, the definition of trading success. Consistency in your trading may allow you to trade for a living or, in other words, to live exclusively from your trading profits—but you must invest in yourself first. In this particular case, that investment is a long-term commitment to learn the right trading concepts and blend your knowledge with trading experience.

If you want something, go get it. Period.

Real Trading Example: It took me five years to become a profitable trader and almost another five years to become extremely consistent. If I had come across the right trading material and concepts earlier, I'm sure the learning curve would have been far shorter. This course will give you the materials and concepts I wish I'd had early in my career.

A trader once said, "Well, trading is easy. It is the research, design, coding, testing, and execution that is hard." This is a funny way of looking at the absolute truth. So commit yourself—take this course seriously, and plan to work hard.

Homework: Which part of the day (or week) will you devote to taking this course and thinking thoroughly about these topics? Create a routine. Write it down!

Chapter 2

* * *

Developing a Trading Strategy

If it works, it works. Different types of trading strategies or styles have their followers. In fact, some traders believe in their particular style with such fervor that they consider all others inferior. I disagree. For example, I am a systematic futures day trader. I obviously consider systematic day trading to be the best strategy for independent traders who trade for a living. But I also know people who are very good swing traders of both stocks and indexes or who are excellent option traders. So again, anything that makes money consistently works.

Each trader must develop his or her own trading methodology. This requires hard work. Attempting to use other traders' ideas instead of developing your own methodologies will not make you successful.

Every great trader who has ever lived has developed his or her approach by adequately using certain market techniques that apply to a particular market at a particular time. One commonality among all successful traders is that they are in sync with the markets.

One of the best S&P futures traders of all time wrote on his trading desk, "In any market, in any market vehicle, in any time frame that you are trading, there is always a way to make money. Find it!" You must learn to think this way in order to develop the right trading strategies for the markets you are trading. Keep asking yourself, "What is working, and what is not working?" If you can embed this way of thinking about the markets, you will suddenly be playing at a higher level.

Where would you place yourself in this table? (Use a *D* for discretionary trading or an *S* for systematic trading.)

	Stocks	ETFs	Other Futures	Options	Index Futures	Forex
High Frequency trader (HFT)						
Day Trader			s			
Short-term Trader						
Medium-term Trader						
Long-term Trader						
Investor						

I filled the table with my own answer. At the end of this course, you should be ready to place your *S* in a single box as well.

2.1 Choosing a Trading Style

A trader must make the effort to master a very specific type of trading method or trading vehicle. The trader who does so has a much better chance of success than does one who dabbles in many different things and never makes much progress. *Specialize*—do not be a jack-of-all-trades, master of none.

The successful market participants I know have spent a great deal of effort idealizing, researching, and refining a unique approach to trading that captures an enduring bias in the markets.

There are a few very important concepts here:

1. Spending effort thinking about a unique approach
2. Researching that unique approach and refining it into a tradable strategy
3. Focusing that effort into finding an enduring bias in the current marketplace

In this process of finding your trading niche, you must ask yourself questions, then go looking for the answers. What works in this market? What do I need to add or subtract to make this method work better? Which market instrument is best to buy weakness and sell strength? These are a few examples of introductory questions in developing a method.

If you follow one course of action until you are successful, you cultivate expertise. If you pursue many strategies simultaneously, it's difficult to master any. I define trading success as being able to win consistently in the markets and being able to provide a steady return month in and month out in a way that enables you to trade for a living.

To sum things up, what you want is to get in the habit of making the same trades over and over again. All you need is one pattern to make a living. In starting a new business or investing in financial markets, outstanding results derive from original thinking—great successes are, to a large degree, a function of creativity.

Basic Trading Personality

There is one important question you must answer about yourself that will guide you through the process of choosing a trading strategy that's right for you and your trading personality: Are you an *innie* (a trader who likes constant action, who loves being involved in the markets constantly) or an *outie* (a trader who likes to wait for a perfect setup to come by)?

Personally, I am definitely an outie—I do not have the fear of missing moves and being left out of the market, as most innie traders do, but I hate being in a trade that's losing money. I stay out of the market for most of the trading session and strike only when I have what I consider to be a perfect setup.

The important point here is that if you are an innie, you may want to try something such as trading Bollinger Bands; selling strength and buying weakness; or being almost always in the market, either on the long side or the short side. If you are an outie and planning to day-trade the markets, you may want to focus on capturing a move per day. This basic personality trait is an important factor in determining what type of trading strategy you should develop.

Real Trading Example: I am a futures day trader who goes in and out of the market a few times per trading session, making a bit of money several times a day. After trying other methods and styles for years, this is where I have found my consistent profitability. It fits me well.

Homework: What type of trader are you? Do you consider yourself an *innie* or an *outie*?

When you try different styles, different time frames, and different asset classes, you will reach your niche, finding both the time frame and trading instrument that best fit you. It's a long journey for many, but it is surely a very rewarding one. It takes time to learn trading, but it takes a little *more* time to reconcile that trading knowledge with who you are.

The Best Type of Strategy to Develop

You should try to develop a strategy that strikes a good balance between giving you an expectation of making money over the longer term and finding you a lot of opportunities to trade. The strategy must have a *positive expectancy* (where trading profits are positive and big enough to cover commission and slippage) and also a high *opportunity* (the number of signals this particular strategy generates). The higher the better, considering it has a positive expectancy.

2.2 Research and Testing

An aspiring successful trader is not allowed to have market opinions unless he or she has extensively backtested something or studied the charts. Doing either of these indicates the perfect state of mind for a consistently winning trader.

A winning trader can have an opinion on the future direction of prices only when it's based on study. Without study, having market opinions, especially when based on analysis produced by other traders, is a very expensive habit. Traders should develop opinions only after studying what markets have tended to do when in similar situations in the past (for example, crossing a moving average, being up X days in a row, or closing above or below a Bollinger Band).

The more you test different trading ideas, the more opportunity there is for good luck to show up in your tests. Testing trading ideas is like digging for gold or looking for crude oil in deep waters. The more trading ideas you test, the better your chances of finding patterns that can be traded profitably.

I would say that for each twenty or thirty trading ideas that I test, maybe *one* will be valid and later used for mechanical trading. Obviously it is not easy to uncover good trading patterns—if it were, everyone would find them and negate one another's edges. A keen eye for patterns, good analytical skills, and a lot of hard work are mandatory to find something really good for you to work with.

When a trader is testing patterns and systems, he or she will find lots of things that do not work. A trader should expect to spend dozens of hours testing ideas and not finding anything really useful. Persistence is key, and it is also very important to keep building on what you already have. If you start with an idea and test it, you will reach conclusions that may lead your next testing in a slightly new direction. You should keep following this process until you reach your goal, finding a tradable pattern that can be used in a systematic approach to the markets.

Backtesting Your Trading Ideas

What is *backtesting*? It's the process of testing a strategy using historical market data. The idea is to validate a trading approach before a trader commits real money to it. By doing a backtest, a trader simulates the trading results of a particular system or strategy over a chosen interval (one month or one year, for example) and evaluates them to decide if the levels of risk and profitability are good for trading or if further adjustments will be needed.

Where can you backtest your ideas?

There are a few sources for backtesting trading ideas. If you are using end-of-day data, you can download the data to Excel and work it from there (you can download the open, close, high, and low prices for US stocks from Google Finance).

If you want to test trading concepts with trading indicators, you can use the websites Finviz or ETFreplay. For more complex trading ideas, you must learn to code using TradeStation's EasyLanguage. You should invest some time learning to work with EasyLanguage, as it is the most sophisticated backtesting tool available for individual investors.

Real Trading Example: How do I do my own backtesting? Well, for the more complex stuff, I have hired a computer-science expert who codes my trading ideas and tests them. For the simple stuff, I backtest by hand. If it is not a very complicated backtest, you should do it by hand as well, as you will learn the most this way.

Homework: Generate a simple trading idea and backtest it.

(Example: If Apple [AAPL] or any other stock of your choice traded down three, four, five, or six consecutive days, and it is trading above the ten-, twenty-, or fifty-day simple moving average, what are the average returns if you buy at the close after two, three, five, or ten days? Go back a few years in your study and compile the results. Do the test with a few stocks or ETFs, test other variations, and work the concept with your own input.)

Real Trading Example: Here's what I have found to be the most productive for doing market research: Crunch numbers for forty to fifty minutes and then take a ten-minute break. This way, when you come back for more research and analysis, your brain has had the time to synthesize the market data, focus on what should be emphasized, and be clear on what should be tossed away. So many times I've spent hours and hours doing research, only to get lost in the data.

Homework: Your task for now is to think about and develop a low-risk idea that can be translated into a trading setup. There are two essential elements to developing a low-risk idea: the first is patience (because you will probably need to think of a few ideas before having one that qualifies), and the second one is risk control.

When I created this exercise for a seminar I gave a few years ago, I decided to participate too. This is what I came up with at the time:

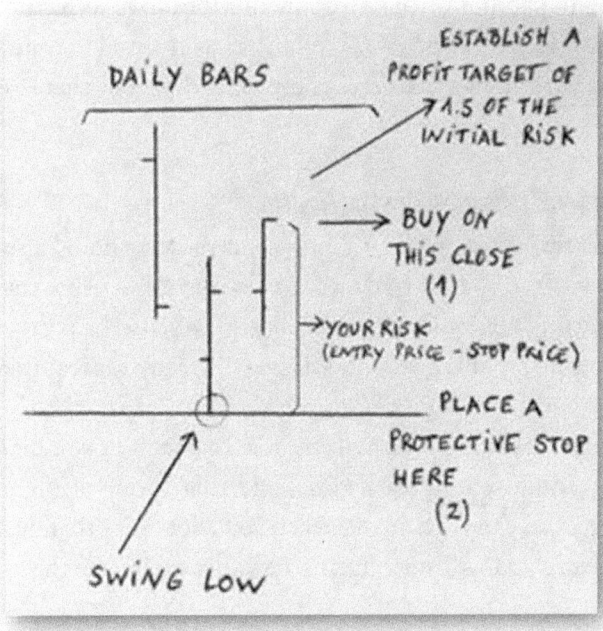

A System for All Markets?

Every trader who wants to develop a trading system has this question: Should I develop a trading system for a specific market, or should I develop a robust trading system that works across several different markets?

There are two options: developing a specific trading methodology or a widely applicable trading system. The first is a system expected to work only in a specific market, whereas the second is an all-terrain system designed to work across many markets.

My approach is to create a system for a particular market; if it happens to work, I might try to apply it to different markets. But when I idealize it, I am thinking about what may be a good system for a market that has certain types of characteristics (e.g., volatility, price persistence, liquidity, and opening and closing hours). For example, if I am thinking about how to trade a big-cap, low-growth US stock, I will certainly try to apply a different framework than if I am trying to capture price swings in an innovative tech stock. They have very different price patterns, so a system that works well for one type of stock will not work with stocks that have completely different characteristics.

Backtesting, Forward Testing, and Constant Monitoring

After you backtest a system or a trading concept, you should also forward test it with live data. You should trade it for a few days in a paper-trading account before committing real money to it. Doing so will also help you validate your backtesting results, making sure the strategy is ready for real trading.

Also, by live testing it, you will be able to watch how a market reacts to a particular trading setup in real time, and that is one of the most valuable trading lessons you can take. It will teach you a lot more than just backtesting it would, because you will start having new ideas to refine the system.

Real Trading Example: After something that looks really good comes out of a backtest, I like to trade it with a fifth of my normal size for a week or two. (I am talking about very short-term systems.) This lets me test the waters, gain confidence, and see if I may have missed something important—all habits I highly recommend.

Homework: Pick one market and watch it every day for a month. Get to know that market inside out. Gain a deep understanding of how it moves; watch it throughout the day, and get in sync with its rhythm, its range, and how it reacts to new intraday lows and highs. By watching only one market and not listening to headline news, you will slowly but surely become an expert in price patterns—the only thing that really pays in trading. Try it out.

Conclusion

Backtesting the market not only gives you an ability to get a feel for how your approach would have behaved in the past, but it also allows you to stress test it to find out if it suits your trading personality. It allows you to stress test yourself against your system's behavior.

When you backtest a trading idea or strategy, do not look at only the aggregate data (e.g., number of winners, number of losers, average win, average loss, profit factor [PF], or maximum drawdown). Try to learn how the system operates on a trade-by-trade basis. How would you feel if you actually *had* traded that system in real time through all those trades? Plot an equity curve and analyze the drawdowns. How many losses in a row did you get? How many consecutive months was the system unable to make any money? These are the key aspects I check when testing new ideas.

Even though the system may have a decent overall performance, it may not be a good fit for your trading goals or trading psychology.

2.3 Trading with an Edge

This may sound a bit harsh, but if you trade without a proven trading edge, your sole purpose in the markets is to create liquidity for good traders to sell into. This is not what you are trading for, is it?

So What Is a Trading Edge?

A trading edge is present when you can anticipate the evolution of the market for a specific period after specified market conditions have been met. This means if we trade that setup a number of times, we will be able to capture the edge and translate it into monetary terms. Traders must learn to think like casino operators—all casino operators have to do is keep the odds in their favor and have a large enough number of plays for their edges to have the opportunity to work.

A trader must adhere to the types of trades that tend to work—or in other words, types of trades that work more often than not—and play them as often as possible. Some trades will be winners, and some trades will be losers; as in the casino business, however, all that counts is the bottom line, not the results of each individual play by the casino's customers. Traders must embrace this trading concept if they want to perform at a very high level.

How Should Traders Start Looking for a Trading Edge?

One way to start looking for an edge is to locate entry points where there is a greater probability that the market will move in a particular direction within your desired time frame. Basically, a successful system is the combination of a successful entry, a successful exit signal, and a position-sizing technique that tells you how many units to buy or sell.

The best way to start evaluating a trading idea is to test its entry signal. Is the signal associated with a higher-than-normal probability of a market move in the desired direction? Test the entry rule with a time-exit rule only. Does it generate more wins than losses exiting the trade after three or ten days? If the entry is good enough, then study potential exits to associate with that particular entry criteria.

Most Trading Edges Are Paper-Thin

Another important point about trading edges is that most are paper-thin. Even the very best of traders have relatively small edges, but they can exploit them to big profits. Most trading edges show a positive but low expectancy— they make on average just a few ticks per trade. This means traders really need to trade them very efficiently and must have the discipline to trade every signal without second-guessing their trading edge (more on how to do that in "The Mental Game," chapter 3).

Real Trading Example: I recently tested a system on the British pound futures, and while it had a winning rate of 57 percent and an average win similar to the average loss, it gained on average only 2.8 ticks per trade. Considering the commission on that contract, the real edge was just 2.1 ticks per trade. With such a narrow edge, good execution is the key to winning money; a sloppy trader may even *lose* money using this strategy, due to its razor-thin edge.

Losing Streaks

Having a trading edge does not mean you won't have losing streaks. This is another very important point: Even if you have a winning methodology, you can be exposed to a big streak of losing trades. As every moment in the market is unique, just because you had two, three, or five losses in a row, it does not mean your next trade will be a winner. Consider this next example:

It's been said the longest recorded streak of one color in roulette in casino history happened in 1943, when red won thirty-two times in a row. The gambler's fallacy is that after such a streak of red, black is more likely to hit on the next roll—it's not.

Even the most successful systems need to have rigid risk-management guidelines in order to avoid the risk of ruin after a bad sequence of trades. Having an edge does not mean the edge will work in small samples; actually, there will be periods when even the best of trading edges will show a few consecutive trading losses. Bear that in mind.

Discretionary Traders (How to Know If There Is an Edge Present)

How do you know if you really have a trading edge if you are a discretionary trader? You can see it in the shape of your equity curve. If it shows some consistency of making money without large drawdowns, then over time you can begin to conclude that you have an edge.

People who are very good at trading the markets have a high level of confidence, which is impossible to gain *unless* you have an edge. It's something you have to feel and believe on your own. Unlike in systematic trading, where the metrics of a system prove the system's edge, it is not something that is definitively provable.

If you are able to make money with some consistency, with a good control of your losses, you get to the point where you feel you have an edge, and your equity curve confirms that. You cannot think you have an edge if you lose money for a long time—that is insane!

Even discretionary traders need to have an edge, which does not exist without a methodology. In fact, I have never met anybody with an edge who does not have a very specific methodology.

2.4 Trading Systems

Systems can trade from Sunday night until Friday close…can you?
—David Stendahl, systematic trader

What Is a Trading System?

A trading system is a group of organized thoughts set out in a logical trading plan, which tells you when to buy, sell, and exit and how much to risk in each trade.

Systematic trading is the repeated execution of a trading edge time and time again in a way that makes it possible to consistently exploit that edge and convert it into trading profits. In quantified trading, the outcome of every single trade does not matter—it is the aggregate series of trades that will show your edge and the money.

You should quantify everything you can in your trading. It's the only way to remove what doesn't work and stick to what is making money for you.

Learning How to Trade a System

The best thing anyone can do when starting out is learn how a trend system works. You should try to trade a trend-following trading system for a while. (Check the homework box at the end of this section for details on how to get started on this.) Doing so will teach you one of the most important—though seemingly counterintuitive—concepts that a swing trader, long-term trader, or stock trader has to learn. That concept is to *ride the trend*, letting your profits get large when the market keeps going in your direction and cutting your losses short when the market trades against you.

Besides trading, a system (in this case, any system) teaches you to be disciplined—to have the ability to follow the trading signals, even when you think the market is going to do the opposite of what your system is signaling.

There are many trend-following systems to explore, but if you test one in a relatively short-term time frame, you will generate more signals and learn quicker. Trade small size or even in a paper-trading account while performing this task, as the objective is not to win any money but to learn to follow and execute a trading system flawlessly.

Homework: Trade, for example, a ten-period EMA-crossover system in a volatile instrument in a paper-trading account; your task is to execute flawlessly. Create a log sheet to enter the trades and the P&L.

Systems Help You Avoid Second-Guessing

When we trade a system, we do not need to ask ourselves if we are right or wrong, as trading systems autocorrect if and when they are wrong. Trading systems have entry points, protective stops, and profit targets, three characteristics that leave no real room for second-guessing. But the discretionary trader has to consider the merits of the trading position all the time. The P&L is one of the crudest and probably best indicators of whether the speculator is on the right side of the market. If there are profits, then in market terms, the trader is right. If the trader is losing money, the market is sending a clear message: "You are—at least temporarily—wrong!"

Homework: Your task is to decide which of these two strategies you would choose for your trading and why. For each strategy, I have included the trading results (wins and losses) from a one-month period trading the EURUSD Forex cross.

Strategy 1:

+30, –12, –22, +8, +3, +27, +21, –12, +25, +12, +3, +20, +10, –25, –22

Strategy 2:

+10, +12, +4, –3, –6, +22, –12, +8, +7, +5

What strategy would best suit you and why? Study the results and write down your answer.

My answer: I decided to analyze those strategies through the lenses of the total return, average profit per trade, and profit factor.

Strategy 1:

Total return (sum of all trades): +66 ticks
Profit factor: (sum of winners) / (sum of losses) = 1.71
Average profit per trade: 66 ticks / 15 trades = +4.4 ticks per trade

Strategy 2:

Total return (sum of all trades): +47 ticks
Profit factor: (sum of winners) / (sum of losses) = 3.24
Average profit per trade: 47 ticks / 10 trades = +4.7 ticks per trade

While strategy 1 shows a larger total return than strategy 2 (+66 against +47), my choice would be strategy 2. Why? The profit factor (PF)—the amount of money you gain for every dollar you lose—is way higher, and it has a slightly higher average profit per trade. Given the higher profit factor and average profit per trade, you could leverage strategy 2 to boost the returns. A higher profit-factor ratio means the strategy is far more comfortable to execute, as the trader is experiencing far more gains than losses. It is easier to be efficient and to avoid trading mistakes when working with a strategy that has a high PF ratio. The average profit per trade is very important too, because trading commissions and slippage erode the average profitability of all trading strategies, to some degree. When you have an extra cushion—that is, a higher average profit per trade—you have a little more room to allow for poor executions.

I would end the comparison by plotting an equity curve of each strategy. The smoother the equity curve, the better. After plotting the equity curve, I would look for maximum drawdowns on both strategies on both profitability and time.

2.5 Risk Management

There are two important dimensions to a rigid risk-management regimen. The first and most important question to ask is this: How much of my trading equity will I risk per trade? The second question to consider is how many trades you will allow yourself to have open at any given time.

Avoiding Excessive Risk

Many potentially excellent traders have been ruined because they took too much risk. It is not unusual for wannabe-pro traders to risk five or ten times more than what is considered prudent for aggressive trading.

That being said, excessive risk is lethal, especially in times where the volatility explodes. If you are experiencing those market conditions in your trading, then it is paramount that you reduce the risk by decreasing the trading size to adjust for the increased volatility in the markets.

Size Matters; Size Kills

A very experienced S&P futures floor trader once said, "You can be a very good one-to-five contract trader, but you will be an average ten-contract trader and a terrible twenty-contract trader."

In trading, size really does matter, which means it's crucial to *know* your size. Your efficiency will decrease dramatically the bigger you play. Why? Because you'll be thinking about money all the time. You must trade at a size that's within your present emotional capacity. Expanding trading size is a difficult task, even for the most seasoned traders. The key is to expand size slowly. For instance, if you usually trade 500 shares of a specific stock, you can increase your size to 550, then to 600, and then to 650 shares. Expanding your trading size gradually means giving yourself time to adapt to the new threshold. It's a bit like lifting weights in the gym—you add them slowly, so your body gets used to the additional burden without experiencing any discomfort.

Bear in mind that your bet size controls your emotions. There is a correct trading size for every trader, and finding that size is absolutely essential to success.

When to Become More Aggressive

Many traders ask themselves if and when they should be more aggressive with their trading. My experience tells me that when you are ahead, when your trading is working well, you should think about increasing your trading size—but only slightly. You have the cushion of the recent trading profits to minimize the emotional impact of trading a larger size, but you should still increase your position size by very small increments over time.

Homework: How much risk are you comfortable taking at the present moment? In terms of both money and percentage, what do you consider to be a normal day swing in your account?

A general guideline is to risk less than 1 or 2 percent of your equity per trade. This means that if the trade does not work, your total loss will equal 1 or 2 percent of your trading capital. (For example, if you are trading a $100,000 account, your maximum losses should be in the $1,000–$2,000 range.)

If you are an active trader, you must accept that you might have ten trading losses in a row a few times each year. The question is what your account will look like when they happen. If you are risking 2 percent of your trading capital per trade, you will have a drawdown around 20 percent. In my experience, that's the worst level of drawdown most traders can handle.

2.6 Changing Market Conditions

As an old adage says, "There's no such thing as the goose that lays the golden egg forever." Market conditions *do* change. One of the real skills for a systematic trader is to understand when he or she needs to change a trading system or its parameters, adapting it—or even when to abandon it altogether and develop a new one.

Traders work very hard to find a trading edge that works, and they'll play it out until it stops working. But they must be prepared for, and even expect, the market to change, and they must know that this unavoidable change may reduce or eliminate their trading edge. That is why it's so important to look for new ideas all the time and to always be testing new systems and patterns— doing so means you'll have a backlog of trading edges to work with if or when your current one loses efficiency or stops working.

One strategy I find useful is to compare the short-run metrics to the long-run metrics to measure a system's health in terms of profitability. This is one of my favorite trading practices. I am always comparing the short-term performance, distribution of trades, and risk metrics of my trading systems to their long-term metrics. I want them to be as constant as possible, because in trading, you do not need a large edge to run a successful trading business—you need, instead, to have a *consistent* edge.

I like to compare the year-to-date metrics (average tick per trade, total dollar win) with the metrics over the last three months and over the last month. What I do is look for evidence of significant deterioration in a particular system. If a system deteriorates too much, I will stop using it until its performance is back in line with its historical data—that is, if it *ever* recovers those metrics, because often a system's deterioration is not temporary.

Be aware that the market may change from time to time and that you may need to adjust your trading edge accordingly or even develop a new one. Charles Darwin said it's not the strongest or the most intelligent who survive; it's those who can best manage change. This is very relevant for trading, as the need to always be in sync with what the market is doing implies an openness to change.

2.7 Repetitive Trading Patterns

Markets are repetitive. In its purest form, this game is simply trading repetitive patterns, which makes it imperative that the trader finds those patterns in the market. It is from this discovery that a trader will start building a trading strategy. What repetitions do *you* see in the markets? A trained eye will spot many trading patterns, because experience really helps the trader to start looking to the right things. One good shortcut is to write down a few trading ideas, then backtest them intensively across trading instruments and time frames.

Again, one of the most important skills you can have as a trader is the ability to perceive patterns in the market. Train yourself to think in these terms: What happens after *X* happens? If *Y* happens, then I should look for *Z*. Learn to quantify what you are seeing. Every trader needs to develop this skill, as finding reliable market patterns is the trademark of a successful trader.

Homework: The most successful traders are always looking for new patterns, and the best way to find them is to look at the charts. Study a few charts (e.g., daily charts [or intraday charts, if you are looking to day-trade]) and look for a pattern. See what seems to be working. Look at the candlesticks, and look at an indicator. Immerse yourself in the charts for a couple of hours. Take notes. Test the ideas that look the most promising to you right now.

Developing a Trading Strategy: Final Thoughts

In order to become consistent winners, traders must focus on three important points.

First, traders need an edge. They need to find a strategy that will produce more profits than losses over a series of trades. These edges can be found via extensive backtesting of the markets or via trial and error. Throughout the years, I have found edges both ways.

Second, traders need consistency. Successful traders gravitate toward a single approach, a single trading methodology. They aim to be the best traders in that niche. Besides, you must execute your plan day in and day out, consistently.

Third, traders need to manage risk and avoid ruin. You must avoid the risk of ruin, the risk of having a series of losses that will deplete or destroy your trading capital. You must plan for a string of losses and find a risk-per-trade metric that allows you to overcome several different scenarios of consecutive losses. Can you handle ten losses in a row without having a substantial drawdown?

There are also two kinds of traders who fail to find success: those who cannot adapt and those who cannot focus and exploit their edges in markets. Of course, it is hard enough to find a tradable, consistent edge that puts the odds in your favor. But after you reach that point, you must accomplish two other things. The first one is the laser focus—you must be focused on exploiting that edge and not be distracted by other market temptations, such as trading outside of your well-defined edge. The second one, in my personal opinion and based on many years of trading experience, is the most difficult challenge a consistently winning trader faces. That challenge is answering these questions:

* Is my trading edge still working?
* Is it still a valid trading edge, even after a two- or three-week losing period?
* Should I change the parameters?
* Should I look for a new trading edge to replace this one? Do I need a new trading system with a new concept behind it?

There is no perfect way to address these issues, but I will tell you what I do when faced with these dilemmas. I draw the equity curve for my trades using that edge/system/methodology, and I check whether there is a sudden trend change in that equity curve. Sometimes, it's just something that has happened a few times in the past, and I do not need to worry about it. I am always looking for new systems and new edges, and I spend about ninety minutes a day researching the markets. Sometimes I am just refining my current methods, but at others, I'm looking for something brand-new in case I find myself in the situation of having to change my core trading edges.

Chapter 3

The Mental Game

Having a trading edge is mandatory. All the mental strengths in the world will not make you a profitable trader if you lack a trading edge. But having a trading edge is not enough if you don't have the mental skills to play that edge and extract money from the markets by executing it flawlessly. That is very hard to do, but it's a skill you must learn.

3.1 Trading with Confidence

In trading, confidence must be tempered with prudence. Confidence *not* tempered with prudence is an accident waiting to happen. In our industry, the impossible happens about twice a year. Even when a trader is fully confident about a trading methodology or is having a fantastic winning streak with very low downside volatility trading his or her system, the trader has to guard against black-swan events. Always risk less than you'd previously planned to. You will not regret this if you trade long enough.

What Type of Confidence Do You Need?

Of course, trading with confidence does not mean you need *blind* confidence in each trade. You need enough confidence in your overall trading ability to put on a variety of trades—in other words, you need confidence in your overall methodology.

While you should not expect much of any given trade you make, you must be very confident in your ability to come out ahead after a series of trades. What are the most important factors for that state of mind? You need confidence in your trading edge, the ability to execute your trading plan flawlessly, and the experience to blend it all and make the necessary adjustments going forward—because a winning methodology is always a work in progress. As the market's dynamics change, you may need to adjust the parameters, or even some building blocks, of your method (e.g., market selection, entries, exits, position sizing, risk management), as we have seen in section 2.6.

You need enough confidence to keep trading your method no matter the outcome of the last few trades. Some trades will be immediate losers, while others will be winners. The main point here is that any particular trade can be a failure; it's the edge across trades that makes you successful.

Why Do Some Traders Lack Confidence in Their Trading?

There are two major causes of lack of trading confidence:

1. Not putting in the work. When we try to borrow ideas from others, we're less likely to understand those ideas deeply. The process of generating an idea independently ensures that the idea makes sense to us. That gives us staying power during temporary periods of adverse price action.
2. Negative self-talk. Don't be too hard on yourself. Understand that trading mastery is a slow process and that you must be patient with yourself. Great things take time to accomplish. You must be your own number-one supporter and the first one who really believes it's possible to become a successful trader, because most will try to discourage you. When we focus on everything we could have done better and

everything we did wrong, we create a lot of small failure experiences for ourselves over time. Our self-talk reflects our relationship with ourselves.

Homework: Do you have confidence in your trading right now? Do you need to work a bit more on finding or refining your trading style and edge?

3.2 The Right Trading Mind-Set

The best traders do not experience fear, hesitation, or anxiety when trading. They remain cool, composed, and relaxed. How is it possible?

Accepting and Embracing Risk, Avoiding Fear

Successful traders are unsusceptible to the common fears that negatively affect other traders. Successful traders accept the risk of every trade, which keeps them from experiencing fear while trading. They trust in their skills and trading edge, and they size the trades according to their emotional risk tolerance. The best traders simply aren't afraid, and they can go in and out of the markets effortlessly. If you still experience fear or any type of discomfort, such as recurring hesitation while trading, you still have work to do on yourself— something is not completely right yet.

Learn to trust your edge, learn to trust your methodology, and trade at a size that is comfortable to you. Keep adjusting until you can trade without fear. As I mentioned earlier, if you are experiencing fear while trading, something is wrong. Conversely, you should not feel overexcited either—you should be conducting your trading calmly in every circumstance.

Embracing Consistency

You need to be consistent, always. If you find you are sometimes buying and sometimes selling in identical market situations, then there is something very wrong with the way you are approaching the markets. Your reactions to similar trading situations must be consistent. You need to wait for your setups to develop, then act on them consistently. You cannot buy strength one day and buy weakness the next; that is random trading, and random trading will surely result in losses. You must be able to identify clearly whether conditions are met for you to execute your trade. If they are, then execute flawlessly by playing the entry, the exit, and the position sizing according to the plan. Perhaps the most important component in a trader's ability to accumulate money over long periods is having a great belief in his or her own consistency.

Ultimate Emotional Control

After each trading day, your significant other, your kids, and your friends should not know just from looking at you whether you made or lost money. You must get to the point where no one can tell how you did on any given day. Building the ability to keep your trading-related emotions from seeping into other areas of your life implies you have achieved the ultimate emotional control, and doing so shows the right trading mind-set.

Getting Comfortable with Discomfort and Imperfection

Most traders are obsessed with being right on every single trade and get frustrated when a trade does not go so well. Even the very best traders have many trades that turn out to be losses, and that is OK. A trader who aims to be consistently profitable over the long term cannot be obsessed with single trades. But the very best traders not only have many losing trades—that's just part of the game—but also from time to time may make a trading mistake. (I define a "trading mistake" as not following the rules, the predefined trading plan.) The most successful traders are OK with that too. They embrace imperfection, and they accept some bad luck that may also intrude from time to time. Consistently winning traders do not get frustrated with those infrequent minor mistakes; they're able to rebound quickly and get their trading efficiency back without generating a self-perpetuating cycle of trading mistakes. I have seen many traders make a mistake to cover for a previous mistake—I call these "self-perpetuating mistakes." You must avoid them at all costs.

Avoiding Burnout

Trading is intense and very time- and energy-consuming, and many traders may develop some kind of burnout from time to time. This tends to occur when key components of well-being are absent from our daily lives.

To sustain a healthy mental state, we need to experience happiness and pleasure. We also need a sense of satisfaction, the experience of doing meaningful things. In trading terms, this can be developing a trading strategy focused on making money in the long term. It can also be using some trading profits to help a cause you care about.

Another important point is to stay energized. You should work out regularly, eat a healthy diet, and avoid negativity in your daily life.

The most important factor of all to avoid burnout, however, is to have a solid social structure. We all need to experience closeness and support, so don't forget to invest in your relationships and close family and friends. (Obviously this might also include connecting with some good traders.)

Homework: Consider this question: Am I being consistent in my trading? Be brutally honest in your answer—if the answer is no, create a nice-looking Post-it to remind yourself to be more aware of this. You might even consider buying word stamps and writing "BE CONSISTENT" on your Post-it. You will never forget this experience, and the lesson likely will sink in.

3.3 Admitting and Correcting Mistakes

There's an old Wall Street adage that says no trade is a total loss if you have learned something from it. That is true. Your greatest error as a trader may be not admitting your mistakes, because then you can't correct them; without correcting your mistakes, you will never excel at trading—or at anything, for that matter.

Whatever mistakes you are making in your trading, you must come clean about them. You must admit your mistakes, accept them as necessary for your development as a trader, and try to correct them.

You may make the same mistake a few times before the lesson finally sinks in. That's normal, as it has happened to most successful traders along the way to consistent profitability. You can use the Post-it technique I mentioned earlier to highlight the recurring mistakes; this may help you create a sense of alertness and try to minimize those mistakes until they are gone for good.

Homework: Take a few hours now to go through some of your recent trading mistakes. Study yourself by asking these questions:

* What were your biggest mistakes?
* Have you learned those lessons yet?
* Have you made some recurring mistakes?
* What are you doing wrong?
* Are you letting losses get away from you?
* Are you grabbing profits too quickly?
* Are you jumping around to different strategies?
* Are you trading different markets and not becoming an expert in any?
* Are you trading too big and making fear-based mistakes?
* Are you trading with money you can't afford to lose?
* Do you think you don't deserve the money?
* Are you trying to avoid trading losses at any cost?

These questions cover 95 percent of all trading mistakes. Answer them. Write a brief summary of how you plan to eliminate the mistakes that may have been plaguing your trading.

Elite performers in every field spend a lot of time reviewing their work as part of ongoing learning. An honest review is mandatory, and for that to be possible, you must be willing not only to admit but also to learn from your mistakes in order to become a better, more consistent trader.

Your equity curve tells all about the viability of your current trading methodology. If your equity curve is not going from the lower left to the upper right with only small fluctuations, you need to keep making adjustments to your trading and correcting your mistakes.

3.4 How to Think about Individual Trades

Most traders focus too much on the outcome of the trade they are currently in. This is a big mistake and the source of most unnecessary trading losses.

Each trade should be seen as one trade of the next twenty or fifty the trader is going to make. Many of those will be losses, but many will be winners. The results of those bigger sequences—and not the trade-by-trade outcomes—are what really matter. Imagine this sequence of trades, all taken using the same trading system (all amounts in USD):

+350, –200, +450, –600, +820, +340, +220

Should you be worried about trade number two when it was losing $200? Should you give it a little more room before closing the trade at the $200 loss and risk losing $900 or $2,000 on that trade? Or even worse, should you risk not taking trades three through seven because you are still stuck in the second trade trying to avoid a loss? Does that make any sense to you?

What is the importance of trade number two or trade number four in the overall sequence? They are just pieces of the puzzle. If you are confident that your method is good, you should not be very worried about trying to turn a losing trade into something else, thereby risking creating a huge loss for yourself. You must learn to accept the trade as it is, winner or loser, and move on with your business.

Thinking in these terms will reduce the pressure to make the current trade work. This way, the common trading mistakes, such as giving the trade a little more room to work; denying market information that the trade is not working; moving stop-losses, or even worse, averaging down, will happen *less frequently*, and at one point they will just not happen anymore—then you will smile and think about these words. You can thank me later.

If you trade with a proven trading edge (where the odds are in your favor over a series of trades), every loss will be overcome by a string of winning trades that will bring your equity curve back to a new high. So why should you be bothered by a loss? There is no good reason for you to be bothered.

The outcome of a single trade is random. Again, you must focus on capturing a trading edge over a series of trades. Your focus must be on the trading process itself and not on the random distribution of wins and losses common in every trading methodology. This is one of the most important concepts of this trading course.

If your current trade turns out to be a winner, forget about it and move on. If your trade turns out to be a loser, you should forget it even quicker. As long as you did the right thing—followed your trading strategy, entered the trade on the entry signal, traded it a predefined position size, and respected the exit rules—you should pat yourself on the back.

Do not let yourself give in to the emotional roller coaster of placing too much importance on each individual win or loss. Wins and losses are a part of the game. Accept that, and your trading stress will be greatly reduced—you will feel much better about your work.

Plan of Action: Think of each trade as one of the next fifty trades you'll make. If you start thinking in terms of those next fifty trades, all of a sudden you'll have made any single trade seem very inconsequential. In this context, who cares if a particular trade is a winner or a loser? It's just another trade, one of many to follow.

You may have a trading strategy that has a 70 percent win rate, but that does not mean you can't have a few losing trades in a row—each trade is independent from the others. Just because you lost on the last trade, you should not hesitate to go into the market the next time your trading setup gives you an entry signal. The reverse is also true: just because you had three winners in a row, that doesn't mean you should go all-in for the next setup or that you should avoid it because after three wins in a row, you fear your next trade will be a loser. Learn to operate like a robot.

Consider this example of a strategy that has produced three small losses in a row but still is profitable:

Trade 1: –12; Trade 2: –22; Trade 3: –14; Trade 4: 100.

In this case, your profit factor is 100 / (12 + 22 + 14) = 2.08, meaning that for every dollar you lost, you won $2.08.

Every moment in the market is unique, as the buyers and sellers are never the same and don't react in the same way. And that is what a market is: the collective behavior of buyers and sellers. You should not expect anything from the market when you enter a trade, except for the market to express itself in some way and move up or down.

Avoiding the Recency Bias

Every trader I've come across throughout the years has suffered from the recency bias, although to different degrees and in varying forms. The recency bias is the tendency traders have to weigh recent profits and losses more than they value earlier profits and losses. Average traders' feelings likely will reflect how their last two or three trades went. If a trader had three winners, he or she will be feeling great, but if the last few trades showed a loss, the trader will be feeling down and uncertain about his or her trading. Another good example is this: if you lost $1,000 yesterday, you would be more upset about that than you would be about another $1,000 you might have lost in a similar trade six months ago. Why is that? Does it make any sense?

Traders must fight these deeply seated instincts. A trade is just a trade, and the outcome of every single trade is almost random. The professional trader must concentrate on the process of executing the selected strategy over a series of trades, confident that after a decent number of trades, the trading edge will produce more profits than losses. So my advice is this: Do not focus on the results of the last few trades. Concentrate instead on your monthly and yearly trading goals.

3.5 Avoiding Self-Sabotage

The principal reason for self-sabotage is thinking you do not deserve the success or money. In order to be a successful trader, you must feel deserving. To do that, you must forgive yourself and your trading mistakes and accept that you deserve success. Feeling deserving also means having put down the work and feeling you deserve to be paid for the research efforts you have made.

If you spent dozens or hundreds of hours taking this course, researching the markets while looking for a distinctive trading edge, you will feel like you deserve to win, right? That is part of the commitment, and it is essential to long-lasting profitability in your trading.

This is typically the inside struggle. But there is also an outside element to feeling deserving, which relates to how you interact with others. If you improve yourself—if you are a better person for others and are more tolerant with yourself—you will feel better about yourself. You will feel an inner peace, and your results will likely improve. (And so will your life.)

A famous poker player once said, "The best way to get better at poker is to get better at everything and let poker rise with the tide." It is the same with trading. Work on yourself, and you'll be making an effort to be a better person to everyone and everything surrounding you.

The fulcral point here is that you must feel good about yourself. This also means making peace with your past, knowing you are responsible for your happiness, learning not to be constantly comparing your life with others', and learning to live your life in peace. Sometimes, especially in this endeavor, one must not think too much nor take oneself too seriously. Learn to laugh more often, and everything will look rosier.

Homework: Consider these questions and work through these tasks:

* Whose day will you improve today by taking a deliberate action?
* How many people will you be able to make laugh this week?
* Which trader friend will you help by showing him or her how to think about his or her trading?
* Make it a family routine to watch a funny movie every week.

These ideas will get you started, but no one knows your life better than you do. Find a few more tasks to add to this list that are specific to your life and loved ones.

3.6 Overtrading

Perhaps a large number of your poor trades were triggered by your desire to do *something*. If there is nothing to do, then do nothing. A few years ago, I had already perfected most of my trading systems and had a smooth equity curve, but from time to time, I felt urged to play a special situation in a stock or in the indexes. Those operations only added volatility to my trading and drained emotional capital. That was the last issue I had to fix to become a stress-free, consistently profitable trader.

If you trade for a living, it is very important not only to be consistently profitable (because you have to pay the bills), but also to stay relaxed and confident at all times. You must be confident that you will always (not most of the time) be able to act in your own best interest. Avoid those temptations to place a side bet when you are already well ahead in your learning curve.

Almost every trader has the tendency to overtrade. The ability to sit on their hands and wait patiently for the best setup is a rare skill among novice traders—it's hard to be in front of the screen and resist the temptation to trade, because the markets *are* always tempting you. There is always a *theme du jour* on CNBC or on Bloomberg, or perhaps a trader you follow on Twitter and respect mentioned a stock or an ETF.

The most successful traders have learned to isolate themselves from all the trading noise. And trading noise is *every* piece of information that does not constitute an integral part of your trading methodology or system.

One Answer to Overtrading

One of the answers to overtrading is *not* to discipline yourself to make fewer trades, but rather to channel that energy toward creative and constructive activities such as market research.

Every trader suffers from overtrading from time to time. In my case, when I am in a drawdown, I want to get back to new equity highs as quickly as possible. That may lead to the temptation of overtrading, when I feel inclined to make a few more trades than my trading plan tells me to in normal conditions; however, I have found a good defense against overtrading. That is to study the markets further, do some extra historical backtesting, and test slight variations on my systems. I just try to find some little things that are better than what I am doing at the moment, and I coach myself to wait for those trades to come along and be able to climb back up to all-time highs.

Learn to use *your* energy in a more productive way too. Once you reach the consistent-winner plateau, you will be less tempted to make extra trades—you will be more than happy just to trade your well-crafted plan.

3.7 Self-Coaching

Learn to be your own trading coach. Take notes on Post-its and attach them to your trading screen or leave them on your trading desk. Consider what messages are the most important for you at your current stage as a trader. What do you think you need to be focusing on?

Here are a few practical examples:

1. One trader might be focused on expanding his trading size without losing its efficiency. His note could say, "Focus on playing the setups as efficiently as you can. Money will follow."
2. Another trader may be fighting overtrading. Her note could read, "Play only your best setups. Don't be easily distracted; it does not pay."

Be creative—do not be afraid of creating a true piece of art with your Post-its! Eventually, if the messages are repeated enough times in enough ways, they will become part of a trader's self-talk and a natural part of performance.

How to Keep Getting Better at Trading: Study Yourself!

If you are a performance athlete of trading, you have to spend as much time studying yourself and your performance as you spend studying markets. Continuous performance improvement in trading begins with the collection of trading metrics. There are many similarities between professional sports and trading, one of which is that statistics are key to performance improvement. We must measure everything we can about our trading. The most basic metrics are the percentages of winners and losers, the average size of winners and losers, and the profit factor of every single trading strategy.

You must also keep track of how much you are up or down year to date and the details of your monthly performance. Your task is to calculate these simple metrics about your trading and to find where you need to improve.

We must measure everything we can about your trading. Try to segment your trades in every possible way, including the following:

* Analyze your long entries for the last year, then compare them with your short-selling entries. Can you conclude from the data that you are a better buyer than seller?
* Now segment them by size. Did your smaller positions work better than the larger ones? Or was it the other way around?
* Segment the trades by instrument traded. Do you trade a few select stocks better than you do others? Do you trade indexes or stocks better? Do you feel more comfortable trading Forex, for example? What seems to be your best trading instrument?

One hard lesson you will have to learn as a trader is to understand and accept what you do best in the market. There are day traders, short-term traders, and investors. Short-term-oriented traders are very good at pattern recognition and enjoy fast action. Long-term investors are usually good at analysis or long-term trend-following techniques. Regarding risk, you will find that there are aggressive risk takers and balanced risk traders who pursue a very smooth equity curve in detriment of absolute return. These are fundamental differences of cognitive and personality style. You will find your success by capitalizing on your distinctive strengths. That means you must know, understand, and embrace your strengths.

Real Trading Example: Regarding this last section, almost every trader seems to have a trading instrument he or she trades better. In my case, I am more efficient trading the Euro futures and the gold futures. I am less efficient trading the Nasdaq futures. So I try to play more of what works best for me, and you should do the same.

Homework: Your task is to segment your trades, study them, and find what steps can improve your trading immediately.

Study Your Best Trades

A great trading practice is to study your best trades and how you made money in them. Study your worst trades and the factors that made them lose money. Did you make a mistake? Were these trades part of the plan? Is there any way to avoid those trades in the future?

We're most likely to be consistently profitable if we're consistently mindful of our strengths and vulnerabilities. Know yourself—be aware of your core trading strengths and weaknesses. The important question here is that all traders have their trading niche, the type of trades they tend to do best because they are a good fit to their trading personalities. Some traders are good stock pickers, some traders are good at cutting losses, some traders are good at riding winners, some traders are good in finding short-term market correlations and relative strength, and some may be excellent system developers.

Study your past trades, and try to see if there is a type of trade that stands out in terms of profitability. You need to find your niche and become an expert at it. I do not know any successful trader who is good in more than one trading style. Focus on what you do best.

Homework: Find your best and worst trades for the last year and debrief them. Learn everything you can about what went right and wrong with those trades.

3.8 Flawless Execution

Without the right level of discipline, you will not follow any trading system—no matter how good it is—long enough to make money, and this is why successful trading is so hard to achieve. Not only it is difficult to master the analytical part of trading and the computer knowledge to design a profitable trading system, but you must also possess the mental skills to follow the system.

Many traders have the tendency to jump from one system to another at the slightest evidence of performance deterioration. That is a huge mistake. You must have the discipline to follow a methodology or system for a reasonable period. You need a big trading sample to confirm whether the system is trading according to your expectations. If you are a day trader, I would consider a sample size of fifty to one hundred trades before considering any adjustments. For longer time frames, I would use a slightly lower sample size before making any changes to your system or methodology. Make that commitment and avoid the temptation of jumping around parameters and systems.

Reality Check: How good are you at applying your trading plan? Can you execute your trades flawlessly, obeying the protective stops and targets you predetermined? In your last twenty trades, how many had a flawless execution?

Flawless execution of any strategy is the toughest part for a trader, because it requires mental skills that are the most difficult to learn and incorporate into your functional level. To execute flawlessly, you must have absolute confidence in your trading methodology and also trade at your right trading size. You cannot feel any discomfort with the outcome of your trade: If it loses, it loses. It cannot have second guesses or hard feelings. It's just the way it is. Some trades will be winners; some will be losers. Do not resist this absolute truth of trading, because that is unavoidable.

All traders have execution problems to some extent. Another reason for that is that in the heat of the battle, it is easier to make mistakes. Write on a sticker, "I trust myself and my edge. I execute flawlessly." These shortcuts are very helpful for keeping you committed to a trading principle.

Homework: Create a few Post-its that may increase your self-awareness in the heat of the battle. Place them in or on your trading desk.

Patience

Patience in trading has a double meaning: (1) waiting for the right trades, and (2) staying with trades that are working. I have often referred to traders' need to wait patiently for the right trading setups. I am adding a new dimension to what it really means to be patient in trading because, if you are in the right trade, you must also be patient to stay with that trade, especially if you are a rules-based discretionary trader. It's hard to find a trade that works right from the start. When traders find themselves in that optimal situation, they must take full advantage of it.

Trading Rules and Trading Habits

The right trading behaviors must start as rules, but they will slowly evolve into trading habits. When traders are still looking for their trading niche, that very setup that will be the trademark of what they do, they need a rigid set of rules to structure their behavior. That list should be written, printed, and placed in a visible place by the trading desk. As you evolve as a trader, you incorporate your strategy into every fiber of your being. It becomes a habit, and suddenly there's no rigidity at all; you just trade your methodologies and do not distract yourself with any trading information unrelated to your trading setup.

3.9 How to Manage Drawdowns

A drawdown is the peak-to-trough decline during a specific period suffered by a trading account. A drawdown is normally expressed as the percentage between the peak and the subsequent trough.

Every trader goes through losing streaks and the inevitable drawdowns. Sometimes these drawdowns are extended, either in time or in the amount of money lost. And while some traders bounce back from these losses, there are many who don't. So how should you think in order to be resilient enough to come back from a period of trading adversity?

Being Resilient

I cannot think of a characteristic more important to long-term trading success than psychological resilience, which is the ability to maintain high levels of functioning throughout the exposure to very stressful conditions. You must expect to have drawdowns from time to time, and resilient traders are aware there will be losing periods in their trading. They expect this to happen from time to time, and they know what to do in order to overcome it.

If suddenly your strategy seems to have stopped working in the current market conditions, scale back on your trading and adapt your trading strategies to the current market conditions. Study the market harder and more deeply than ever. This will surely help in solving the problem that may have caused the drawdown.

Winning traders know they have to be in sync with the markets. This is *resilience*.

Studying Drawdowns

We must study the size and duration of the equity drawdowns in our account. While every trader has his or her own risk tolerance, drawdowns should be confined to 20–25 percent of the trading account. Otherwise, traders will have a mountain to climb to get back into new equity highs. You should measure the size (in percentage terms and dollar amount) and also the duration in days.

Another very important risk metric is the distribution of the daily returns of your trading account. This will immediately show you the risk you are taking in your account and also your propensity to change your risk profile when you are doing well and when you are trading poorly.

The Right Mind-Set to Overcome a Drawdown

You should not be risking more when you are in a drawdown. Be patient; if your strategy is good, time is your best friend, and if you execute flawlessly, you will be making new equity highs soon.

Homework: Complete the following steps to guide yourself to a positive mind-set:

1. Create a Post-it to place on your trading desk that will redirect you to this chapter when you are in a drawdown.
2. If you have a $100,000 account, how much could you lose in your worst drawdown that would keep you trading with the same energy and efficiency?
3. If your account went to $90,000, would you still maintain the same energy and discipline? And if it went to $65,000, how would you feel about it?
4. If you think in these terms, you will begin to know what type of drawdowns you can withstand. Knowing this, you also know what kinds of risks you can take.

The Best Way to Overcome a Drawdown Is to Trust Your Method

If you don't trust yourself or your methods, you will not find the emotional resilience to weather periods of loss. Even when you have found your trading niche and have a proven trading edge to trade the markets with a positive expectancy, you will have to know how to go through periods of losses. As you know, drawdowns are inevitable in any trading strategy. You must be prepared to deal with them without self-destructing. Many traders increase their risk when facing an uncomfortable drawdown. You must avoid that at all costs.

Only you will know your niche well enough to evaluate whether market conditions are still benign for your methodology. If they are, and obviously this a tough call to make for traders of all levels, you must keep trading and wait for your equity curve to start rising again. In periods of drawdown, I tend to do more backtests of my systems, comparing the current parameters with the historical parameters—in other words, I am trying to keep my confidence in my methods high. A second thing that helps me when in a drawdown is to look at previous drawdowns and how well I got out of them by just continuing to trade the same way. Finally, another technique I have found helpful is doing more of the things I love *other* than trading when in a drawdown that is affecting me. Read a good book, ride your bike often, or go to the movies. Buy a few fine wines for your cellar, or go watch live sports. There are a million things to do, but you must get rid of the negative energy consuming you. You can't trade if you are feeling worried or stressed.

Real Trading Example: To conclude the trading game chapter, I want to share with you my answer to a question raised by an interviewer, "13 Professional Traders Answer: How Do You Deal with Emotions in Your Trading?" about how I deal with emotions in my trading. My answer was as follows:

Well, this is the million-dollar question, isn't it? The answer is obviously very complex, but I will try to simplify it a bit. First of all, one must be absolutely confident in one's trading edge. I often have the metrics of my trading systems on my desk, and I stare at them throughout the session. This way, I know that on average I will have those trading results. The key is not to get very emotionally involved in every trade you make, but rather to think of being efficient in a series of trades—for example, in every trade you will make in a day, in a week, or in a month, depending on your strategy and time frame.

Another "trick" is to have Trading Cards on my desk, to help me focus on particular trading topics.

Basically, I have my trading desk reinforcing my trading skills, communicating with me in a way that helps me remain efficient in my trading and act in my own best interest.

Again, if you are very confident in your strategy and in your ability to execute it flawlessly, you have nothing to fear. Time will take care of itself, and profits will come in. But even if the idea is relatively simple and easy to understand, reaching this state of mind requires brains, perseverance, thousands of trades in experience, and the right trading beliefs—I could write a book on *this* subject alone.

Chapter 4

Markets: What Works and What Doesn't

This chapter is designed to help you search for the right trading tools (such as indicators and techniques) to develop and sustain your trading edge. In short, it is a summary of what approaches have a better chance of working in the markets you are trading, both from my own experience and from the experience of the dozens of successful traders I've come across throughout my trading career.

4.1 Being in Sync with the Market

A trader must try to be *with* the market itself and not trying to beat it. A trader must try to do what the market is doing. This seems obvious, but I suspect you have had issues with this before, as is the case with most traders. Many traders find it very difficult to trade by trying to be in sync with what the market is doing.

The most successful swing traders I have met seem to share this commonality: they just go with the flow. Surfers will surely relate to this, as they wait for the best waves to ride, and they obviously do not consider surfing against the waves—that would be impossible. A very successful trader once said, "If you act in sync with the market, trading can make you rich. If you choose to argue with the market, it will surely make you poor." I will add this: it will make you poor, frustrated, and angry.

The task of a trader is to find a way to be in sync with the market. Remember when I wrote early in the course that a very successful trader once said that in any market, in any time frame, there is a way to make money, and your job as a trader is to find it? This means the trader should not apply predetermined conditions to the market and see if they work in real time but rather should invert the process and see what is working in the market; then he or she should try to design a few sets of rules that will profit from what the market has been doing.

Homework: Pick a market in which you have an interest. What trading indicators have been working the best in your selected time frame?

4.2 Market Type: Momentum, Mean Reverting

Mean reverting means that after going up, the market tends to consolidate or give back some gains, and after trading down, it tends to recover and trade up. Momentum in markets happens when a market moves quickly in one particular direction without meaningful retracements. This is the most critical assessment you will have to make about a market, because the approaches that will work in one type of market likely will fail miserably in another.

For example, the E-mini S&P 500 future is a classical mean-reverting market, as it creates a lot of market noise, back-and-forth price action, for every move it makes. In contrast, the DAX futures, which is also an index future, is more trend following and driven by momentum.

Before you approach any market to develop a trading strategy, you must ask this basic question: Is this a mean-reverting market, or is it a momentum market? The way to trade a momentum market is diametrically opposed to the way you should trade a back-and-forth, slow-moving market. If it is a momentum market, then you have to adapt to its speed, and you can explore strategies to benefit from momentum, such as breakout trading.

You must know the basic behavior of your market to design a strategy to trade it. In the E-mini S&P 500 futures contract, a mean-reverting strategy will tend to work better over the long term. Index products are really not trending ones, though this comes with some notable exceptions. They do trend—everything trends—but they don't trend the majority of the time. There are many mean-reverting strategies to test, but one that comes to mind is using moving averages (using a certain move above or below a moving average as a trigger to a mean-reverting trade to the average). Other techniques that tend to work well in slow range-bound markets are envelopes and bands, such as the Bollinger Bands.

Real Trading Example: Everything I design in my trading systems is around mean-reversion strategies. The reason I prefer mean reversion to trend trading is that, as a day trader, I need a few setups a day to trade, and there are more chances for capturing a few moves a day with mean-reverting techniques. If you are looking to be a full-time trader in the S&P 500 futures or on the index exchange-traded funds, you should start by looking into mean-reverting strategies, because these markets tend to mean revert. Actually, most days on the S&P 500 index are range days (more on this topic on section 4.3).

Where to Look for Momentum, Trends

Markets that are newer, less developed, and have less participation likely will show stronger trends. If you rank all the index markets in the world, you will find that the US markets are the noisiest. In this case, noise is measured by how much back-and-forth movement there is, given the net change over time.

This is a useful piece of information if you are developing a trading strategy or deciding how you trade a particular market. The markets with the most noise are best traded with short-term mean reversion, and the markets with the least noise are trend following and can be traded with classical trend-following approaches, such as n-day highs (lows) breakout systems or even a moving-average crossover. Again, this can be very useful information to refining your strategy.

Momentum can also be found in new technology stocks, which are disrupting a particular market and can create big trends. It is not unusual for this kind of stock to double or triple in a couple of years. Some commodities also tend to show momentum characteristics.

4.3 Indicators and Trading Techniques

The hard truth is that there are many traders who use tools and indicators that do not work, but they keep using them because they do not know they don't work. Many traders are using tools that don't really have a statistical edge. Adam Grimes, a successful systematic trader, pointed out recently three trading tools that do not work but are widely popular among traders: Gann analysis, Elliot wave theory, and Fibonacci ratios. My experience points in the same direction: traders should not base their trading on these techniques. Instead, I have included below some techniques I consider potentially useful to incorporate in a viable trading strategy, given the proper context.

The Two-Hundred-Day Moving Average

Paul Tudor Jones once said, "My metric for everything I look at is the two-hundred-day moving average of closing prices." It is very rare to get a trading lesson from one of the greatest traders of all time, and Paul Tudor Jones has probably made more trades than any other active hedge-fund manager. The two-hundred-day simple moving average is by far the most popular technical indicator among medium- and long-term stock traders. If the asset is trading above the two-hundred-day moving average, it is considered to be "healthy," while if it is trading below, it is considered to be a "sick" asset.

One other interesting point Tudor Jones made was that throughout his multidecade trading career, he saw so many stocks go to zero, and for that reason, traders need a line of defense against catastrophe. You don't need a better weapon than this one to prevent a catastrophic loss. If a stock or an asset is trading below the two-hundred-day moving average, you just do not play it from the long side.

Figure 1: Example of a stock trading above the two-hundred-day moving average. (Chart courtesy of StockCharts.com.)

Figure 2: Example of a stock trading below the two-hundred-day moving average. (Chart courtesy of StockCharts.com.)

The Ten-Day Exponential Moving Average

Pit Bull trader Marty Schwartz used to trade using the ten-day exponential moving average (EMA), mapping the market as a green light if the price was trading above the ten-day line and a red light if the price was trading below the ten-day line.

The most successful traders have maps that represent the territory, the markets. They tend to see the market in a unique way, through their lenses. In this case, the ten-day exponential moving average of S&P futures market marked the bullish territory (when prices are trading above the line), where a trader should consider entering long positions, and the zone below the ten-day EMA is considered bearish territory, where a trader should consider only short positions.

Figure 3: Example of a situation where the S&P 500 Index ETF is trading above the ten-day exponential moving average. (Chart courtesy of StockCharts.com.)

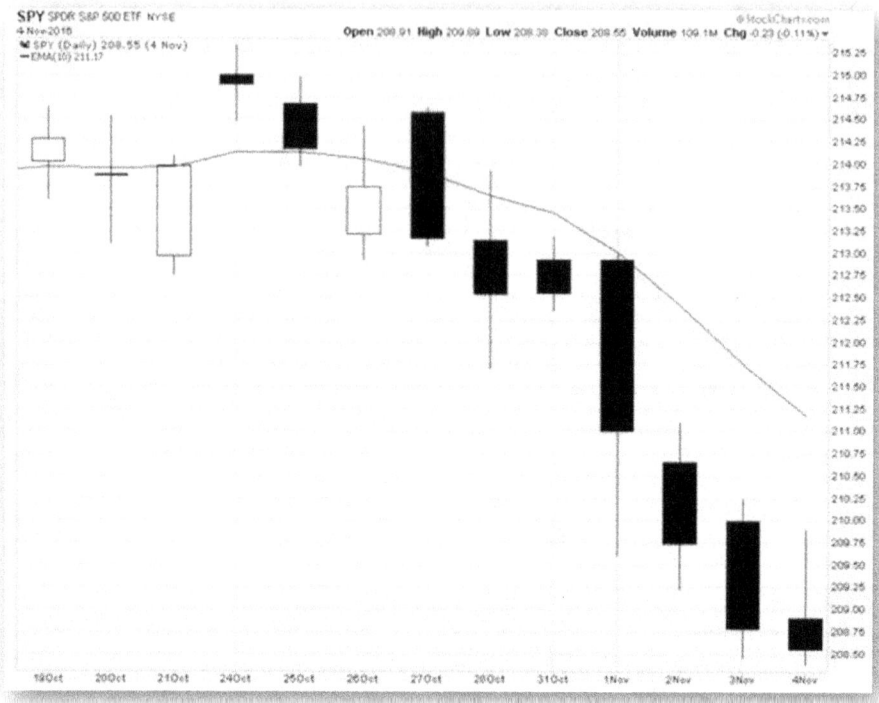

Figure 4: Example of a situation where the S&P 500 Index ETF is trading below the ten-day exponential moving average. (Chart courtesy of StockCharts.com.)

Playing Market Trends

When a new market comes on board, like a country with a stock index, it is very easy to trade with a very short term trend program. They represent what our markets were in the 1960s and 1970s.

—Perry Kaufman, trading systems expert

With very low participation, mostly commercials, these new markets tend to have very strong trends, and you can watch them as they get participation over a few years—they become less easy to trade with a short-term trend, and you have to extend the period of your trend out a little to avoid the noise developing in that market. If you rank all the stock markets in the world, you will find that the US markets are the noisiest, followed by the European markets, Asian markets, and Latin American markets. Sometimes we should look for trading opportunities where most traders aren't looking, as the opportunities to make money may be in the less obvious markets.

How to Use Overbought or Oversold Levels (RSI, Stochastics)

A good idea may be to generally look to buy oversold levels in rising markets and sell overbought levels in falling ones. Many successful traders like to use overbought and oversold conditions in these terms, which means respecting the longer-term trend of the asset.

Figure 5: Example of a Newmont Mining (NEM) chart with both RSI and Stochastics and a fifty-day simple moving average. (Chart courtesy of StockCharts.com.)

Chart Analysis

Charts do not forecast prices, but they may indicate the path of least resistance for future price direction and provide an excellent risk-management tool. For example, a chart may suggest a good place to insert your stop-loss, thus limiting the maximum number of points a particular trade may move against you (e.g., on a swing low or swing high or on a moving average).

When you look at a chart, you should try to determine the line of least resistance, where price is flowing, and what levels it is moving away from or rejecting. Always be open-minded when looking at a chart.

Studying Volume

Volume is the fuel of rising stocks. Stocks and markets in general can fall under their own weight but need new buyers to push prices higher. Learn to watch and study volume on your stocks. Seeing the volume rise when the stock is in an uptrend is a confirmation of the move.

Seasonality: Day of Month

One of the most consistent trends you are going to find is monthly seasonal days. An easy place to look for a trading edge is to study the monthly seasonality in the stock indexes by studying the performance early in the month, mid-month, and also end of month. The returns are not equally distributed: they tend to be much higher on average at the beginning and end of the month.

Homework: This is an easy study to run, as you need only closing prices and Excel. What are the strongest days of the month over the last three or five years? In the study, and for simplicity, use only days when the markets are open. For example, if the first trading day of the month falls on January 3, that day is day one in your study.

Day Trading: Where Are the Trend Days?

Trend days are labeled as sessions where the market opens near the lows and closes near the highs or opens near the highs and closes on the lows. They are basically days where the market goes in one direction all day long.

Studies show that trend days in the S&P futures happened, on average, between 10 and 15 percent of trading days (two or three days per month) over the last ten years. The rest of the trading sessions are mostly range days, where the market just trades back and forth.

Using Volatility as a Trend Filter

What can volatility per se tell you about the current state of the market? When markets start to have big down days, big up days, and a lot of dramatic intraday reversals, it is likely we are in a down trend. A bull market tends to be smooth, slow-paced, and even boring, while bear markets or corrections are emotional and volatile.

No Real Movement of Importance Ends in One Day or in One Week

As they say, "Rome wasn't built in a day." Traders are often too anxious to close a successful trade and move to a new trading opportunity. What happens is that traders may catch the early stages of a meaningful trend, be satisfied with a little profit, and feel tempted to close that trade prematurely. But no real move of importance ends in one day or one week—this is true for stock plays, currencies, and commodities. If your trade is working, if you were able to catch a trend in its early stages, if the trade is showing you a profit right from the start, don't be too anxious to cash in. It's very likely that more money is coming to you from that very trade.

Figure 6: Example of a multimonth move higher in Citigroup
(C). (Chart courtesy of StockCharts.com.)

Gaps

Here's an interesting trading concept for you to study further. A gap is the space between prices on a chart that occurs when the price of an asset makes a sharp move up or down with no trading occurring between the last closing price and the new opening price. Steve Burns, a very experienced stocks and stock-indexes swing trader, says his research and experience tell him that if a gap does not fill in the first hour or in the first ninety minutes of trading, it stands, and a further move in the direction of the gap is likely. As he puts it, "If a gap doesn't fill in the first hour and a half, it just tends to get worse through the day."

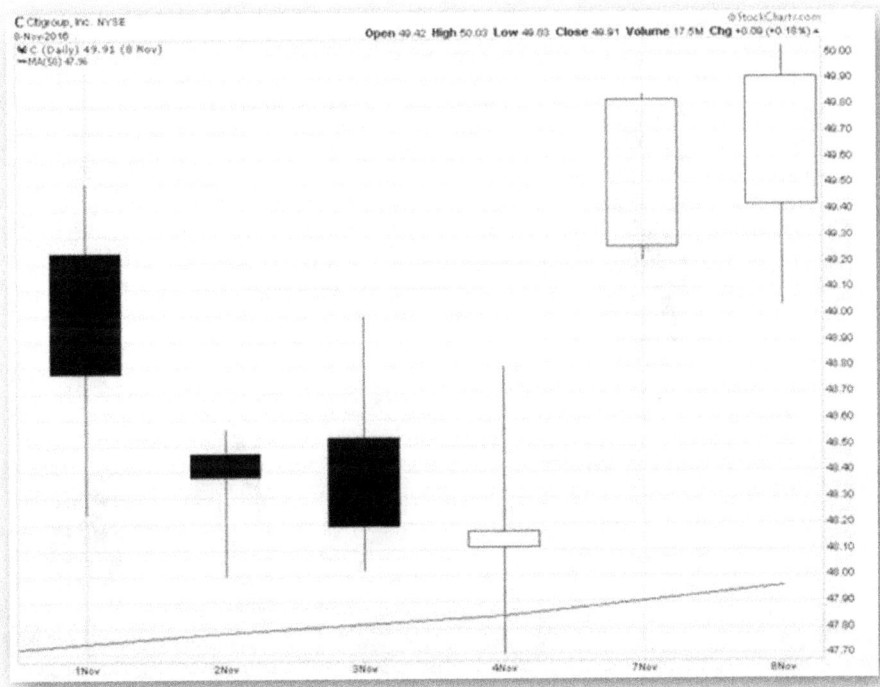

Figure 7: Example of an up gap in Citigroup (C). (Chart courtesy of StockCharts.com.)

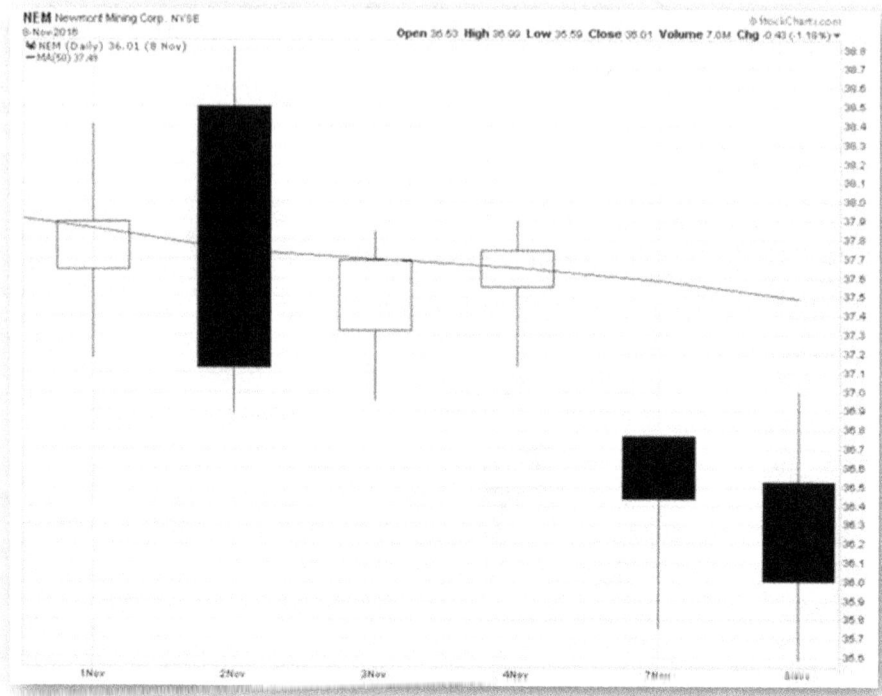

Figure 8: Example of a down gap in Newmont Mining
(NEM). (Chart courtesy of StockCharts.com.)

4.4 How to Trade Stocks

As many traders have a preference for stock trading, I have dedicated this section to stocks trading. Traders who play stocks have an advantage over traders who play other markets: they have thousands of stocks to choose from. I have assembled a few very important principles that I consider to be important to trade stocks successfully.

Know Your Stocks' Habits and Personalities

It is very important to have a deep knowledge of every traded instrument, and stock traders should have a short list of stocks to follow. Every stock acts differently, as they have their own rhythms and personalities.

As a rule of thumb, following anything from ten to twenty stocks is probably adequate. This way, your perception of supports, resistances, and relative strengths will be much better. This method will help you find the stocks that are more suitable for your trading style.

A Good Stock Goes Up

William O'Neill once said, "My philosophy is that all stocks are bad. There are no good stocks unless they go up in price. If they go down instead, you have to cut your losses fast." This reminds me of another quote I came across a few years ago: "Stocks must be treated like employees; if they don't perform, fire them!"

Figure 9: Example of an uptrending stock—a multimonth chart of 3M (MMM). (Chart courtesy of StockCharts.com.)

You should not a buy a stock when it is dropping, even if it has good fundamentals. Do not be interested in falling stocks, period. And if a stock is falling alongside a rising stock market, that is an even worse scenario. If anything, it might be a signal to sell the stock short while that negative relative strength plays out.

The only sound reason for buying a stock is that it is rising in price. If that is not happening, no other reason is worth considering. It is that simple. This principle alone will save you a lot of headaches and money.

The Great Paradox

One of the big paradoxes in trading, and particularly in stocks, is that what is trending up is usually undervalued and what is trending down is usually overvalued. This is a very important concept. So, if a stock you own is acting right (going up), you should not be in a hurry to take profits. What seems too high and risky to the majority generally goes higher, and what seems low and cheap generally goes lower. Anyone with an interest in the stock market has probably realized this already.

Finding Strong Stocks (Relative Strength)

Most successful stock traders seem to operate in a similar way: they find the strongest stocks, and they ride them higher. Relative strength is an important concept for stock traders, as many want to own the strongest stocks in the strongest sectors. This is the typical profile of the successful short- to intermediate-term stock trader. Using this principle, sometimes the best stock to buy is the one you already own. Focus on the leaders and learn how to get the most from them. When you trade stocks and hold a few stocks in your portfolio, you can assess the relative strength of those stocks against the general market and against themselves. Successful stock traders learn to press the winners, adding to their best-performing stocks. They know the strongest stocks tend to get stronger.

Trading Price and Price Only

Knowledge of the companies you trade may not help you, and it can actually hurt you. This is a very provocative thought, but I tend to agree with it. If one trades a stock without knowing anything (or almost anything) about it, what will happen? You will have to focus exclusively on the price flow, on how it is reacting relative to the market. You will be doing trading in its purest form. It is obviously a difficult concept to apply to many stocks, but it's an interesting exercise to make the trader focus on price and price alone.

Eyes Wide Shut (until 4:00 p.m.)

If you are a medium- to longer-term trader or investor, try not to follow the price action in the market until after 4:00 p.m. (or until the market closes). This way, you will have a better perspective of what really happened in the market that day than will someone who sat through it and witnessed firsthand all the day's ups and downs. It is easier to spot relative strength or strong stocks when you look only at closing prices. If a stock was down, up, and then down again throughout the day, it sends you multiple signals and data points that are completely useless if you are trying to catch an intermediate-term move. Focus on the essentials, on what is important for your time frame.

Being Patient with Your Winners

Jesse Livermore once said, "As long as a stock is acting right, and the market is right, do not be in a hurry to take profits." If you ask one hundred successful traders to summarize what really works in trading in just one sentence, the vast majority of them will probably say, "Cut your losses short, and let your profits run." If a stock you own keeps going up and acting right, meaning that it is even outpacing the market, you should not be in a hurry to close that speculative commitment. You are riding the right horse, so why would you want to get out of the race?

There's a second important point here. Most stocks are highly correlated to the general market, so it's better for the market to be acting right too for maximizing the success probability of a single stock speculation.

How Many Stocks to Hold

Mark Minervini, a momentum stocks trader, says, "For someone who has a small- to medium-sized account, I would try to get all my money in four, five, or six stocks." This seasoned trader is obviously not a fan of diversification, as it is an impediment to super performance. His philosophy is to expose your portfolio to the best stocks in the market at any moment. Interestingly enough, he considers four to six stocks to be the right number to allow a minimum diversification and at the same time allow a superior trading performance. Another point in favor of having a small number of stocks in your portfolio is that you can move quickly and track them easily. Consider this catastrophic example: You own just four stocks with the same weighting, and one of them gaps down 50 percent overnight. Well, your portfolio will get hit, but it's a 12.5 percent loss. It's a big loss for sure, but it is easily recoverable. If you are holding six stocks with the same weighting in your portfolio, the hit would be a little over 8 percent. So even in a catastrophic event, the losses would be relatively contained.

Is Your Selection Criteria Flawed?

If you find yourself hoping your stocks get back to breakeven repeatedly, or if after you buy a stock, it generally tends to go against you, one of two situations is occurring: either it is not a good market, or your selection criteria are flawed, and you are not picking the right stocks to buy. What tends to happen after you buy a stock? Do you have the impression that after you buy a stock, two or three days after you go in, the stock typically is underwater?

There are two basic reasons for this. The first is that the market is not strong enough for holding long positions. Have you ever heard the Wall Street saying, "A rising tide lifts all boats"? It isn't *exactly* true, but it is a very applicable principle—if the stock market is not strong, it will be difficult to get in stocks and be profitable right away. The second reason is the one to which you must pay even more attention. Are you buying stocks that go against you despite the stock market indexes being strong and rising? That is a major warning sign that you are not picking the right stocks to buy and should start looking for a better entry signal or selection criteria.

The Dangers of Being a Contrarian

In order to win as a contrarian, you need perfect timing and the perfect size. If you do it too small, it's not meaningful, but if you do it too big and your timing is not perfect, you will get in trouble as the stock moves further against you. In other words, you should not be a contrarian trader in stocks. It is a very tough way to make money in the markets.

One of the best indicators of success in a single trade is that the trade is making money right from the gate. Being a contrarian, you will start most trades wrong-footed and losing money. Even the very best contrarian traders have long streaks of unprofitability, and they have difficulty realizing when they are wrong, because the more the price moves against them, the more convinced they get that they are right. That is no way to trade.

How to Use Market Pullbacks to Your Advantage

When a market pulls back hard (in a 5 or 10 percent correction), most stocks will sell off in tandem. But then, when the sell-off stops and the markets begin to turn back up, only the healthier, stronger stocks will head back to their recent highs rapidly. Those are the stocks you want to own in the next leg higher.

The Long-Term Candidate

Warren Buffett says it is far better to buy a wonderful company at a fair price than to buy a fair company at a wonderful price. If you want to buy and hold stocks for the long run, it is much more important to buy a fantastic company, even if you pay a little bit too much for it in the short-term, than it is to find a short-term bargain in an average company. The reason is simple: A fantastic company will keep growing its revenues and earnings over the long run, and the stock likely will keep trending up. If the company is indeed a fantastic one and the price keeps rising and rising, you will not have to worry much about your entry price. When you buy an average company, your timing will be much more important, because you may not have the long-term earnings growth in your favor. Time is the friend of a wonderful company but the enemy of a mediocre one.

Fear the Bear!

In a bear market, most stocks are unsafe. In a bear market or in an aggressive market correction, almost every single stock will be sold, even the strongest ones. For a trader, the safe place in a situation like this is cash.

Chapter 5

Creating the Right Trading Structure

If you organize yourself, you organize your trading. The very best traders are obsessed with organization. Successful traders have a solid trading routine, write a trading journal, have a written business plan that guides their trading, and are constantly making an effort to learn new things.

5.1 Trading Routines

The best traders have trading habits, daily routines they repeat day after day. Here is an example of a good trading routine that will be suitable to most trading styles:

1. Get out of bed on time and be fully prepared before the market opens.
2. Adhere to the trading plan throughout the day.
3. Execute flawlessly.
4. Respect the predefined risk parameters.
5. Do a complete postsession review.
6. Fill your trades in on the trading-journal log sheet. (I have included a few sample entries below.)

Date	Contract	Size	Entry	Exit	Net	Entry	R	Week-Day	Strategy	P&L
08/Set	GBP	20	15988	15978	10	short	1.00	4	1	$1 250
09/Set	GBP	20	15851	15861	10	long	1.00	5	1	$1 250
09/Set	GBP	20	15851	15854	3	long	0.30	5	2	$375
10/Set	GBP	20	15779	15883	4	long	0.40	6	1	$500

Below I will share a few trading routines I find indispensable to my own trading.

Doing a Daily Debriefing of the Trading Session

Successful traders know that a consistent and systematic review of their daily trading activities is the direct path to growing and improving. After the market closes, I like to take half an hour to debrief my trading session.

These are the questions I ask myself and answer in my trading journal:

* How many trades did I take?
* Did I make any trading mistakes? (I define a "trading mistake" as not following my trading rules.)
* How many points or ticks did I take out of the market?
* Did I spot any new trading pattern interesting enough to study further?
* How was my energy level?
* Did I drink enough water during the day?
* Did I exercise today?
* Did I learn anything new?
* Did I find some interesting articles to read later?
* Did I come across an interesting trading podcast or book?

The best way to improve your trading is to build on what you have already. An incremental improvement each day will make the difference in the medium and long run.

Besides doing a daily debrief of your trading, you must do a more in-depth review of your trading at the end of the month. What is working well in your trading? What adjustments do you need to make going forward?

Real Trading Example: Here is an excerpt from my trading journal of a debrief I did a couple of years ago:

1. I just found that one of the trading instruments where I made the most money last year is showing me a loss after two months of trading. I may need to reevaluate my trading strategy for this instrument or stop trading it for a while. (The futures contract in question is the gold futures contract.)

This was my subsequent answer to the problem:

I decided to keep playing this instrument, because the long-term equity curve is still uptrending with low volatility. There is no evidence of a permanent deterioration of the system's performance by looking at the equity curve. While the short-term performance is relatively poor, I do not think I have enough data to consider that the edge for this particular system has ceased to be active. My decision is to keep trading it but with a smaller size (fewer contracts) for a while.

2. My currency futures trading is as good as it was during the aggregated trading statistics from last year. There is no need to make any changes.

Regarding this specific topic, here is what I wrote:

I decided to increase my trading size slightly in these trading instruments for the next month.

3. On the research front, I found that I have not had a new trading idea that could be translated into a new setup, into the development of a new trading system.

My planned course of action was as follows:

I must dedicate more time to new ideas. I need to spend more hours backtesting some trading ideas that I have already written down in my trading journal. So far, I found one interesting trading setup that I will start running at a small size next week.

Real Trading Example 2: Here is a similar trading review from a very successful trader: "A little while ago, I conducted a review of my winning and losing trades. The best predictor of whether one of my trades was successful surprised me: It was the length of time since I had placed my previous trade. When more time had elapsed between trades, it meant I had waited for everything in my research to line up. Those tended to be the most profitable occasions."

Fill Out a Log Sheet for Every Trade Entry or Exit

The best way to prevent spontaneous trades is to force yourself to fill out a log sheet for every trade entry or exit. Using a spreadsheet to register all your trades is very useful, and you should register all your trades, the entry price, exit price, trade size, and reason to enter and exit the trade. This way it will be harder for traders to insert spontaneous trades that do not fit their trading plan.

Every trader feels an impulse to trade from time to time. The most consistent, seasoned traders have learned to deny those impulses and stick to what is time tested and really works.

Trading Preparation

Successful traders spend more time identifying good trading opportunities than actually putting on and managing trades. Your productivity away from trading is very important for your overall trading success. The time you spend in trading preparation will greatly enhance your probabilities of choosing the right trading setups.

Real Trading Example: I follow about fifty trading systems I have designed, and that consumes most of my trading-related time. I screen, evaluate, and rank them every day. I then decide which systems or setups are most appropriate to trade at any given time. This is the core of my work as a trader; the time I spend executing the trades is relatively small when compared to the time I spend preparing, sorting, and evaluating different trading opportunities.

5.2 Trading Journal

Writing a trading journal is one of the first things trading mentors at prop-trading firms will recommend to their apprentices. The journal is a great way of tracking what we do and why we do it and will also be the most important source of new trading edges, as you will gain the habit of writing your trading ideas based on market observation more often. Keeping notes each trading day about your trades, your results, your new market-related ideas, what you experienced, your doubts, and so forth will solidify your trading experiences, and you will begin to master the fears and self-doubts that affect every trader.

I highly recommend using a trading journal on a daily basis. I have my Moleskine notebook open whenever I am sitting at my trading desk. When something worth noting comes along, I write it down. I may write down a new idea for a trading system, how a particular market has responded to an economic-data release, or a new book to read that I came across while reading an article. It's basically a "best of" list of all the events throughout my day. I highlight things I can use to my advantage later.

After you learn to use your trading journal properly, you will never be able to trade (or work) without one. It is definitely a powerful learning tool. Many traders start using a journal but later succumb to the pressures and demands of daily routines, and the journal takes a backseat. If you want to work with a trading journal, you must feed it daily—even a few times a day. In my experience, it is unusual to find a trader who consistently maintains a journal and uses it to further his or her development.

Some traders favor electronic journals such as Evernote, as they can be accessed from multiple devices and locations and allow users to index topics for later review. I prefer an old-fashioned, well-organized Moleskine and a good pen.

In your journal, you should also keep notes on things that are not directly related to trading but that can have a great impact on your overall performance, such as physical activity and diet or new music to listen to. Other topics that must be constantly monitored in your journal are your trading goals and how you constantly are moving forward toward them.

Homework: Buy the nicest trading journal you can find. Also buy a nice-looking, high-quality pen, and make it a habit to always write your trading-related content with that pen—for good luck.

This is the trading journal I am using right now:

5.3 Business Plan

You need a business plan for your trading. Trading is a business just like any other, and all successful businesses need business plans to guide decisions and operations. When you decide to trade for a living, or if you want trading to be a relevant part of your annual income even if you have another activity, you must treat trading as a business.

You need to have a document that structures and organizes all your trading and everything related to it. I am talking not only about the basics, such as entries, exits, and how much to risk per trade, but also how and when to research the markets, how to keep learning, and where to invest in your trading education. Other important elements will be where to trade from (e.g., whether to set up a home office or rent an office space) and what to do when facing a drawdown, just to mention a few examples.

It will take a lot of time to write your business plan down to its completion, but I guarantee you will see immediate results in your trading. Your business plan must ask all these questions:

1. What is the real motivation behind your trading?
2. What are your trading goals? Measure them in small time frames. For example, what is your weekly/monthly profit goal?
3. What markets are you going to trade? Are you going to trade stocks, Forex, stock-market indexes, commodities, or options? What will your niche be?
4. What is your trading capitalization? How much money do you have available for trading? How much can you afford to lose? This relates to question 2 as well.
5. What conditions must be met for you to enter the market? What are the exit rules?
6. How much risk are you going to take on each trade? Are you going to use the percent-risk model (risking, for example, 1 percent on each trade, meaning that if the trade is a losing trade, you will lose 1 percent of your trading capital) or other risk-management formula?
7. How will you research the markets? How will you learn to backtest the markets? Do you have programming knowledge? How will you

educate yourself in this area? What will your schedule be to study the markets?

8. What are your contingency plans? What if your Internet goes down? Do you have an extra connection? Do you have a spare PC if your computer is not working properly? One of the things I have on *my* contingency plan is batteries for my keyboard and mouse. How can I trade without a working mouse? That may seem like a minor detail, but you must address everything that might affect your trading.

9. What exactly is your methodology? It relates to question 3, but you must also address your time frame (e.g., day-trading, swing trading, stock picker), your style (momentum, value, trend following, indicator based, systematic), and everything else that defines your trading style. I am sure issues will come up that you haven't even thought about.

10. What drawdown will cause you to reevaluate your methodology or trading system? What market conditions may cause you to pause your trading (e.g., volatility, economic-data releases, FOMC meetings, ECB rate decisions)?

11. Where will you be trading from? What equipment do you need (e.g., number of screens and use of a laptop or computer)? How will you pay for that?

12. How will you balance your family life? What trading schedule will be most appropriate for your family life? Tip: develop strategies that allow you to be in harmony with your loved ones.

13. How will you reward yourself (e.g., go on a vacation, buy a new watch, buy a sports car)? When will you offer yourself a reward for trading excellence?

14. Where will you register your trades (e.g., Excel file, trading journal, or other)? How and how often will you analyze your trades (e.g., at the end of the day or over the weekend with the markets closed)? How are you going to signal your trading mistakes? What are you going to do to prevent those mistakes from happening again?

15. What are you going to do when personal problems arise (e.g., illness, divorce, loss of a loved one, financial problems)? When should you stop trading for a while?

I think this list covers most of the issues that, directly or indirectly, may affect your trading. If you can think of more important questions that I haven't mentioned, add them to your business plan.

Homework: Work on those topics. Write them down, print them, and make the pages look like a book. If you haven't written a goal down, it's nothing but a daydream.

5.4 Education and Training

Of course traders need education—they need to be exposed to the right trading concepts, including those taught in this course, and build that knowledge into something that is their own. But trading experience is also vital. I once heard that the most important aspect of becoming a good trader is to trade. Well, it's not that simple. You do need trading experience, but experience is not enough if you lack the knowledge to know what you are looking for in your trading. It's not really that practice makes perfect; rather, *perfect* practice makes perfect. A trader must practice almost as though trying to get better at a sport. He or she must trade, track his or her performance, and evaluate it or find a good trading mentor to coach him or her. Be brutally honest with yourself. One technique I find to be particularly helpful among novice traders is to meet with a trader friend and discuss your trades and trading results—but there is no substitute for structured trading experience.

Remember that investing in the right trading books, courses, and trading conferences will return your investment many, many times.

Below I have included a small list of books I recommend, sorted by trading topic.

For a sneak peek inside the minds of top traders:

1. *Reminiscences of a Stock Operator*, Edwin Lefevre
2. *How to Trade in Stocks*, Jesse Livermore
3. *Market Wizards*, Jack Schwager
4. *The New Market Wizards*, Jack Schwager
5. *Diary of a Professional Commodity Trader*, Peter Brandt
6. *Pit Bull*, Marty Schwartz
7. *How I Made $2,000,000 in the Stock Market*, Nicolas Darvas

For day-trading and swing trading of momentum stocks:

1. *Momo Traders*, Brady Dahl and Nate Michaud
2. *Trade Like a Stock Market Wizard*, Mark Minervini

For medium- to long-term trend-following systems:

1. *Trend Following*, Michael Covel

For gaining more expertise on how to develop automated trading systems:

1. *Algorithmic Trading Systems*, Kevin Davey
2. *Universal Principles*, Brent Penfold

On how to rebound from failure and stay the course:

1. *Rebounders: How Winners Pivot from Setback to Success*, Rick Newman

This last book, unlike the others, is not a trading book. It talks about the art of the comeback, of not letting failure define you. You will learn how to stay with the facts of a situation without being too affected and learn to go in new directions if the first one doesn't work. Newman also covers how to be comfortable with risk, and how to be patient, and how to pull inspiration from those who have already done what you are trying to do. Basically, it is a lesson on how to stay on course.

Homework: Make a list of topics you want to specialize in (e.g., day-trading, candlestick patterns, relative strength). Create a routine to study those topics daily—find half an hour in your day for this task. You may even work on those topics with a close friend who is also into trading. My experience tells me that teamwork really pays off when traders are looking for trading edges and expanding knowledge.

Ask yourself every day, "Is there any small change I can make in my routine, in my working space, or in my trading system that may improve my performance or well-being?"

Chapter 6

Tricks of the Trade

In order to win consistently in trading, you must do everything right. An average trader loses money, so in this profession, you need to be way above average to make consistent money trading the markets. This chapter is about the little details that can make all the difference—as they say, the devil is in the details, right?

How Many Trading Screens Do You Need?

Sometimes simpler is better. Many traders have asked me this question throughout the years, but there is no correct answer, as it depends on your trading style more than anything else. For example, I have one trading desk with two large trading screens, one TV, and an iPad that displays my Twitter feed. As I trade only three or four futures contracts, I don't need to be looking at many different charts.

But for stock traders, it's different. They tend to trade many stocks at a time and need to watch potential setup candidates and run stock scans. For an active swing trader, four to six trading screens may be the right number. I remember reading an interview with Ed Seykota (one of the most successful traders of all time), and he had only one screen, which was turned off during market hours. He updated his positions only after the closing bell. As I've mentioned, there is obviously no one solution that fits all, but you get the general idea.

Don't Be Too Attached to Money

If you have any attachment to money—and who doesn't?—it is very tough to trade correctly. This is one of the lesser-known secrets about trading success. When you are trading, you shouldn't be thinking about the money. You should be thinking in point terms, as if you were playing a game. Of course, that must come after you've designed a business plan and put strict risk-management rules in place, such as not risking more than 1 percent of your capital in a single trade. But when you are trading, executing your trades, and watching the market, you should be thinking only in market terms, not in money terms. You should say to yourself, "I am up twelve points on this stock," and not, "I have a profit of twelve hundred dollars on this trade." Try that approach, and your trading surely will benefit.

Do Not Be Obsessed with the Value of Your Account

You should not be obsessed with the amount you have in your trading account on a trade-by-trade basis. Establish a routine to check your equity once a week—for example, on Fridays—just after the markets close. Traders must focus on doing the right things and following their processes. If all these things are taken care of, money will follow. When traders are too sensitive to the small fluctuations in their trading capital, they are much more susceptible to making mistakes. Forget about money while you are trading, but make sure you are following your risk-management rules while you play the markets. Whenever you catch yourself thinking about your P&L during trading hours, take a brief time-out and go for a walk. During trading hours, you have to be market-focused and not self-focused.

Withdraw Profits and Keep Them Safe

It's very important to start paying yourself once you start being profitable in the market. For every $1,000 you earn in market profits, you should withdraw $200–$300 from your trading account. It will give you a sense of reward, and it will reduce your emotional attachment to any subsequent market losses you may incur in the future.

Don't Ever Average Losses

You have heard this one before, haven't you? Almost every blowup that has occurred in the investment world has involved averaging down. If you are losing money on a trade, the market is telling you you're wrong, and that is all you need to know. Throwing good money after bad to try to turn a losing trade into a break-even trade is not the way to go. Remember that you do not have to make money on every single trade—that is impossible. This means you do not need to make money in your *current* trade.

There are so many trading instruments and so many markets to trade, so why should you be stuck in a trade that is not working? And worse still, why should you average down a losing trade? If you are underwater on the trade, you must think about getting out, not committing more trading capital to it. Be smart—don't beat yourself.

After a Good Run of Profits, Take a Day off as a Reward

Many articles have been written about how to handle losing streaks, but discretionary traders must also learn to manage winning streaks. To avoid burnout and reckless decisions, discretionary traders should take a few days off (even one will do the trick) not only as a reward but also to assimilate the gains and regain perspective before they start trading again.

Learn to Think in Profit-Factor Terms

If there is one trait winning traders share, it is that they all understand losing is part of the game, and they have all learned to lose. Traders must learn to evaluate their trading and methodologies through the lenses of the profit factor:

PF = (dollar amount of winning trades) / (dollar amount of losing trades)

In every system and trading methodology, there are always winners and losers. The important thing is that the sum of the winners is bigger than the sum of the losing trades, but as you trade, you will be adding dollars to both the numerator and the denominator of that ratio. Learn to think in these terms, and a loss will mean only that you will add that particular dollar amount to the denominator.

Good Trades Show Profits Right from the Start

There's a fortune in this sentence. If the real money is made in trades where you start making money right out of the gate, this is a tell about how entry signals should be designed. You should enter the market in the direction it is currently trading in *your* time frame. Winning traders seem to be in sync with the markets most of the time. One of the tricks to being in sync is to do what the market is doing without having the temptation to fight it.

Be Very Selective in Your Trading

Increasing the selectivity of your trades and maximizing your review process will be much better than spending a lot of time in front of the screen.

If you spend more time reviewing your trades and less time actually trading, you will naturally become more selective in your trades, as you will find from studying your own trading patterns what really works best for you.

For the vast majority of traders, the more they trade, the smaller their probabilities of being profitable. The pickiest traders are usually also the best. You don't need to be trading all the time. Learn to be selective; learn to be picky.

I have developed a few dozen trading systems for my own trading. Most of them show a decent profitability over time, but I don't trade them all. I choose only the best three or four trading systems to trade at a given time. Do the same. Select your best setups and focus on those. Your overall profit factor (the sum of your total dollar wins divided by the sum of your total dollar losses) will go way up, and you will save a lot of money in commissions.

If you cut the types of trades you take by two-thirds and focus solely on those that reflect your greatest edge in the market and your greatest trading strengths, and if you were to meaningfully increase the size/risk taken for each of those trades, your overall profitability and risk-adjusted returns would rise significantly. Do you think you are able to do this? If a trader really commits to a particular approach that works, the trading results most likely will get better.

Don't Watch Every Tick If You Are Not a Day Trader

The dangers of watching every tick all day long are basically twofold: (1) overtrading, and (2) the increased probability of prematurely liquidating good positions and settling for a small profit. If your strategy does not require you to watch every single tick, you should not. If you can, automate your strategy with stop-losses and profit targets.

Learn to Test the Waters

This point is valid for discretionary traders. When you have very small, exploratory positions in some stocks, you will learn a lot about how they are acting relative to the market and to their sector. You will be able to determine whether the stock is acting well once it starts rallying or if it stands apart from the other stocks, and then you can really add to a position.

I know many traders who use this technique. They have five or ten small trades in stocks they are looking to play, and when the stock really starts to perform the way it should, they add to their position and ride it higher.

It is much more effective to watch a stock you already own than it is to analyze charts for many different stocks. You will get a feel for when it is ready to break out. Adding to the position once you are involved is much easier, and you'll learn a lot about a position just by having it on.

Do Not Worry about Losing Money—Worry about Losing Your Trading Discipline

When traders are in a trade, they tend to narrow their focus. The only thing a trader tends to think about is the outcome of the trade he or she is in right now. This is especially true if the trade is losing money. The trader's instincts will try everything to keep that trade from being a loser. The trader may add up, average down the trade, temporarily remove the stop, widen the stop, or just stay away from the price action for a couple of days to give the trade some room to breathe. I have seen all these tricks among traders, both novice and experienced. But traders should not be worried about losing money. You win some; you lose some. It's the bottom line that counts.

Traders may lose money, but what they cannot lose is their trading discipline, as it is one of the fundamental assets of any trader. All traders must have confidence in themselves. All traders must believe in the deepest sense that they will do what is best for their own interest all the time, and that is to play according to the predefined plan.

Compound, Compound, Compound

Albert Einstein once said that "compound interest is the eighth wonder of the world. He who understands it earns it. He who doesn't pays it."

Imagine your trading edge has an expected gain of 0.3 percent per trading session. It does not seem like much, does it? Well, if you start with $100,000 and compound it (imagine for the sake of this exercise that you do not withdraw any profits from your account in the first two years of trading activity), after two years (roughly five hundred trading sessions) you would have $447,163. Not bad, right?

Homework: Make a table of compound returns with different percentage returns and time horizons with your current trading capital.

Do Not Risk Money You Cannot Afford to Lose

Never risk money you can't afford to lose; doing so is almost a certain way of guaranteeing you will lose it. Do you know the Wall Street adage "Scared money never wins"? If you are trading with money you can't afford to lose, you will be in a situation that is not conducive to the emotional state required to produce consistent profits in the markets. If you need the money to pay your rent, your mortgage, your credit card, or whatever expenses you have, you should not be risking that money in the markets. You should trade only money you know you will not need in one or two years.

Risk Aversion, Risk-Taking

You will never be a greater risk-taker in the markets if you approach life with a completely different attitude. Nor will you be organized and disciplined in trading if you are disorganized in your day-to-day life. As I explained earlier, this is how becoming a better trader is a path to becoming a better person (and the other way around too). The key takeaway here is that by improving our efficiency in daily tasks outside of trading, we are cementing the skills we need in trading.

Trying to be more disciplined and more organized in your day-to-day activities will help you in your trading. I noticed this many years ago. My trading really improved when I got more organized and disciplined outside my trading. Suddenly, it all fit together, and I am now an organized individual in every field of my life, inside and outside of the trading world.

How to Solve Trading Stress

If you find yourself very stressed over a trade, it probably means you are trading too big a position. Size down. Fear is responsible for nine of every ten trading mistakes. You will experience fear when you are trading too big relative to your present emotional comfort.

When you feel like you can't leave the trading desk, or if you are checking prices on your mobile device every five minutes, those are signals that you are committing too much capital and emotional energy in your current trade.

When traders ask me how they can improve their P&L, I tend to answer, "There are many things you need to work on to improve your overall trading consistency and long-term profitability, but if you want immediate results, you just need to trade smaller."

Courage and Nerves of Steel

Novices frequently assume the best traders stand out because they have courage, nerves of steel, and self-control, but obviously that is not what sets them apart. In order to be a consistently profitable trader, you need to have a proven market edge and trade without fear or recklessness. Recklessness means taking excessive risks because you are on a hot streak and feeling invincible—you must avoid that state of mind.

Now, think about this for a minute: If you are trading without fear, why would you need courage? And if you aren't feeling threatened, why do you need nerves of steel? And if you have a proven trading edge and written trading rules to guide your trading, why would you need superior self-control? Superior trading performance is not an extreme sport; it is not visceral. If anything, it is Zen.

Anything Can Happen in the Markets

In the markets, anything can happen at any time, so it is mandatory to be prepared for anything. What seems impossible happens a lot, and every trader who has been trading for a long time knows as much. So be prepared for anything that may happen, and do not be complacent with any trade, because you never know which one will run away from you and never look back. Remember, a trade is just a trade. Before going into a trade, determine your worst-case scenario. Then nothing really threatening can happen to your trading account.

Real Trading Example: Imagine that a stock you are following is down six days in a row. You cannot think it can't go down seven days in a row. Of course it can—it can go down eight, nine, or ten days in a row, and it can go to zero.

Embrace Simplicity over Complexity

All of us go through periods where we add more factors into our trading strategy and periods where we begin to follow more trading instruments, add more indicators to our trading screen, run extra hours of backtesting research, read more articles, listen to more trading podcasts, and so on. The problem with doing this is that once you've been doing it for a while, you will get distracted, confused, and stressed, and you will lose your best weapon: the laser focus.

In trading you should avoid complexity. For example, trading with too many indicators will cause a complexity that may bring confusion and even paralysis to your trading. I think knowing one indicator inside out and knowing where and when to apply it is better than trying to get the best of three or four indicators at the same time.

Just a final note on this topic: A high-level technical trader needs only a chart and a quiet room to trade. That is simplicity. Traders must be focused on their trading edges and ignore all noise. Stick to your guns.

Do Not Become Obsessed with a Particular Market

It is easy for a trader to become obsessed with a particular market that has delivered a few straight losing trades. The trader may even start to think the market owes him or her something. Of course, this is a bad mental state to enter, but this tends to happen to most traders once in a while. Traders who trade only one market are particularly prone to suffer from this malaise. After three, four, or five losing trades in a row, traders will feel as though they have been fooled by the market. Do not try to recoup losses from a market after such a situation. You are probably just out of sync with that particular market. Look for a fresh trading setup in a different market or a different stock.

You don't have to make it back the way you lost it!

Learn to Know When Not to Trade

Trading is a fifty-fifty split between knowing what not to do and knowing what to do. For example, you learn to avoid scenarios where risk cannot be properly managed. Knowing when not to trade is one of the most important skills for a consistently winning trader. I always try to avoid situations where the market may have a big unpredictable outcome. Some examples are trading just before major economic reports, such as the employment report; trading ahead of the Fed meetings; or trading stocks ahead of earning reports.

Keeping Your Brain in Peak Condition

If you are an athlete, you will do everything to keep your body in peak condition. If you're a world-class trader, keeping your body and brain in peak condition is equally important. There are a few things you can do that will help increase your levels of concentration and alertness. First of all, drink a lot of water during the trading session. Water is essential to keep the brain functioning at a high level. Several studies show that dehydration affects short-term memory, concentration, and even motor skills. I drink about seven glasses of water while at my trading desk.

The second thing you must monitor is your sleep. Sleep restores your brain. Try to have a good sleeping routine; seven to eight hours of good, quality sleep is mandatory. A recent study shows that using your smartphone or tablet just before going to sleep has a very negative impact on the quality of your sleep. Use a classic alarm clock—leave the smartphone charging in the living room.

Third, do not stay seated for long periods. Move around. Take a walk once every hour or two. It will increase your energy levels, your mood, and your creativity—even if it is only a walk to grab a glass of water or a coffee—so move.

Improve Everything in Your Life

The best way to get better at trading is to get better at everything you do in your life and just let trading rise with the tide. In order for your trading to work for you, everything must be in harmony. You need to know the markets and yourself, and you need to keep yourself in optimal mental, physical, emotional, and spiritual condition to make sound decisions and sustain a high energy level. Even a good diet is important for your trading success. Trading is very debilitating in energy terms. You need to compensate that with exercise and hobbies.

Plan a schedule that includes ways to stay fit—physically, mentally and spiritually.

Real Trading Example: I will give you a glimpse of my personal routine and interests outside the trading world.

* In my daily routine, I ride my bike for about half an hour early in the morning, and I play with my kid for about two hours before dinner. I am a big fan of watching soccer, and I collect fine wines.
* I also had a big project recently that included buying and decorating a new condo. That has consumed a lot of my time outside the markets.
* My next big project is to look for a vintage sports car.

That's how I balance my life outside of the markets. I also don't look at the markets and don't stare at screens if I don't need to. It's pointless.

There Is More to Life than Trading

When you work, work. When you play, play. Don't mix the two. All traders need some time away from the screens and the markets—spend quality time with your family, go running, watch sports on TV, or drink a fine wine. You need to create routines for your market activities, but you also need time away from the markets. Live your life, because there is much more to life than trading the markets.

Final Thoughts

I have the impression that successful traders know they are meant to be traders, so they stay the course, no matter how hard it may be in the beginning or how many years they need to really excel at trading. They do not even consider it a job or a career—it is more of a way of life or a calling. They do not get distracted, and they can't be talked out of their mission. They are able to finally get the right trading concepts, and they recognize them when they find them. So they keep on moving forward until they become consistently profitable. This attitude toward trading enables them to gain the immersive pattern-recognition experience that separates them from average traders. If you have finished the course, it is very likely that one day in the not-so-distant future, you will be one of ours. Congratulations!

I think I have highlighted everything important for you to become a consistently winning trader in the markets. I have pointed out directions, and now you must work hard to come up with a trading strategy that is good enough to generate profits and is also a good fit to your trading personality and availability. Your final work for this course will be to answer a few last questions. I recommend you go back to specific topics periodically, as you will always be facing new trading challenges in your effort to become a better trader every day.

Homework: What exactly is your methodology? What defines your trading? Could you explain it in a clear and concise way to another trader? If you cannot answer these questions, you are not ready to risk money in the markets. A trader must be able to write down his or her trading methodology in precise terms.

Appendix A: Interviews with Two Top Traders

I interviewed two very successful traders who share my core trading beliefs about the markets. I have decided not to name the traders in these interviews to avoid distracting the reader. My objective here is to show how great short-term traders think about markets and how they approach their trading business.

Interview One: E-mini S&P Futures Trader

Q: What is your background, and what got you into trading?

A: Well, it's a long story. I think it all started when my parents bought a mutual fund in early 1987 (when I was nine years old) and then I used to follow its quotes every day. Well, as you remember, the 1987 crash came a few months later. So I watched it go down for something like twenty or thirty days in a row…That was my first contact with a market "trend," so I got to know trends when I was around ten years [old]. Then, the passion just evolved, and I remember going to local bank branches to check the Forex quotes with my mother. Remember, I was only ten or eleven years old…

Later, I opened a small trading account, and I traded through college, mostly stocks. I always had a passion for it. I graduated and went to work right away (actually a few months before graduating) on a small brokerage house. It was a fantastic experience, because I was introduced to crowd behavior, mass psychology. The brokerage house had one of those trading rooms where clients placed their trades with the brokers. I learned a lot. There were guys who always called the tops by buying and also called the bottom to perfection by selling their longs…What was even funnier is that other clients knew this, and they exclaimed things like this, "Here come the cold feet. Let's all sell our stocks." It was insane.

Q: Did you ever have a mentor while trading, or do you consider yourself a self-learned trader?

A: Well, I had many inverted mentors, like those clients and one of my former bosses that was always finding reasons to get short even in a runaway bull market. But I learned mostly by myself, by losing money in the market. Those are the best lessons you will ever get. But I also have to thank Jack Schwager for the Wizards series books. They were inspirational, and I read them often even now. Other important "mentor" was of course Jesse Livermore, through his amazing book, *Reminiscences of a Stock Operator*.

Q: Why did you choose to focus on futures and stocks, and which do you trade more of or like better?

A: My playground are E-mini S&P Futures and to a lesser extent Nymex Crude Oil Futures. But I have traded everything under the sun, from German Bunds to Orange Juice Futures. At some point, you need to narrow you focus and become an expert in a couple of trading instruments. I love the E-minis. What I found to be the most difficult to trade is the EURUSD Forex cross. I have been beaten up a few times on it.

Q: If possible, what types of things do you look for when getting into a trade? Is it all technical, or do fundamentals also play a role in your decision-making process?

A: Now, I work with a programmer full-time, so all my trades are based on historical backtesting. It's a very mechanical process, all technical, very short-term-oriented and mostly mean-reverting trading. Now it's a lot more boring than it was when I was a pure discretionary trader that bet the ranch on single trades.

Q: Seeing as you have traded for hedge funds, do the strategies you trade today differ from how you traded within a hedge fund. If so, how are the two trading styles different?

A: I never had the degrees of freedom I wanted to on the institutional front. When I had the money to go solo, I just did. I am having the time of my life.

Q: In your opinion, what are the steps to becoming a successful trader?

A: It's like any sports. Practice makes perfect; there is no other way around it. Of course if you have some natural instincts for this business, it will shorten your learning curve a lot...Reading the best books on trading, especially those that are written by traders will also help a bit. You need three to five years of daily trading practice, of screen time, to become a superior self-sustained trader. Most quit after losing all their money or their nerve.

Q: Do you think successful traders can be taught, or do you think it is a natural thing?

A: Even the guys that have above average ability have to be taught. I think this answers it.

Q: As no trading technique works in all market environments, how do you recognize that a market has changed or a strategy does not work anymore (as opposed to having just a small losing streak, which it seems most traders go through)?

A: It's a natural process. I do not think about changing trading systems every week, or even every month. I may find something new and adjust my trading, or I may change the parameters of some of my models. I don't have a definite response to that question. I think experience teaches us that skill.

Q: Any other thoughts on trading?

A: Practice, trade, track, and evaluate your performance. Commit to it. Don't lie about your trading results to yourself or to others. Take your time; you will get to where you want if you have the time, the patience, and if you don't blow up your account in the process. My experience also tells me that if you have an extra income, apart from trading, you will trade better. Why? Because the pressure will be lower, and as you probably already noticed, trading is a mind game.

Interview Two: Foreign Exchange Trader

Q: How would you describe your trading style?

A: Very opportunistic and short-term oriented. I am out of the market most of the time, and I try to catch one or two moves a day.

Q: What instruments do you trade?

A: I trade currencies, the foreign-exchange markets.

Q: For how long have you been trading that particular strategy?

A: For years now. Maybe five or six years but feels like forever.

Q: What do you think is the most important thing for a trader to succeed in the markets?

A: I am not sure. Passion for trading is important, but I have seen many traders that were passionate and did not make it. Traders always lose in the beginning, and they have to keep going, so a successful trader is definitely a resilient individual. But other thing that I think separates those that quit from those that really make themselves great traders is that at some point, in a crucial stage of their development process, they come across the right material, the right concepts (technical and psychological), and at that point they are ready to embrace those concepts and create a trading strategy that is personal but based on those core trading concepts.

Q: Can you describe your daily routine in a typical trading day?

A: I exercise early in the morning or just go for a walk. Then breakfast and coffee, of course. When I get to my trading desk, I just look at how markets are trading through the overnight session. I check if there is something unusual happening that may force me to adjust my systems or suspend trading for the day altogether. Those days are obviously rare. Then I run my backtests, adjust the system's parameters for the trading session, and monitor the early session. Then I look for an interesting article to read. (I read at least one trading-related article on trading psychology or trading-systems development a day, sometimes a few.) I may try to find a trading podcast to listen to—I get a lot of new ideas for testing just by listening to other traders' methods—or run some extra backtests if I am testing any new trading concept or a variation of something in my repertoire. At the end of the session, I just log the trades into the trading sheet.

Q: What was your biggest trading loss ever? What did you learn from that trade?

A: I never talk about those trades, as I do not want to relieve the experiences of the trader I was back then. They happened before I went fully automated, and I erased them from my memory.

Q: Do you use any classical technical indicators in your trading?

A: No. Most of the trading inputs were designed by me. I am testing a new trading concept that uses MACD, but so far nothing really good came out of it.

Q: Why do you prefer day-trading to longer time frames?

A: If you want to have a smooth equity curve and you have the talents to be a day trader you must go for it. No other strategy will give you risk-adjusted returns that are better than what a very good day trader can achieve.

Q: What are your hobbies? Where do you find pleasure outside of trading?

A: First of all, I never think about trading when I am not working, and I do not even talk about markets with family or friends. I enjoy watching live sports. I love swimming. I also have a side project: I am working on an algo to predict NBA game outcomes, crossing game statistics with betting prices from the sports-betting exchanges. I love math and statistics. I also enjoy reading, and I set myself a target of twenty books a year, but I usually come a bit short, as reading takes a lot of time. I read fiction, nonfiction, and maybe two or three trading books a year, but I try to read those while I am at the trading desk.

Q: When do you plan to retire?

A: I am in my early forties. I plan to work for another forty years. It's fun.

Appendix B: An Example of a Backtesting Study

A good trader must be able to look at hard data, synthetize it, and decide if it fits him. The purpose of this section of the course is not to give you a trading edge but to show you how to structure market research and perform a backtesting analysis. I have decided not to describe a highly complex testing that involves heavy computer-programming skills, like those I normally apply to my trading. Instead, I have decided to test a simple approach using simple inputs—a study you can replicate, expand, and refine.

The first step is to decide what basic trading concept you want to test. I decided to test how short-term weakness is resolved in uptrending securities. So without any type of optimization, I started testing a basic entry with a simple filter, a basic exit, and performed the test in a small sample of liquid financial instruments.

Sample: I decided to create an unbiased small sample of financial instruments for the first round of tests. I tested the ten most active tickers (most active by dollar volume) on December 7, 2016, as listed on the Nasdaq.

Ten Most Active Tickers, Nasdaq:

Apple (AAPL): $3,328,556,490
Powershares QQQ Trust (QQQ): $3,148,258,587
Amazon.com (AMZN): $2,836,231,892
Facebook (FB): $2,583,209,858
Microsoft (MSFT): $1,888,433,822
Alphabet (GOOG): $1,355, 389,561
iShares 20+-Year Treasury Bond ETF (TLT): $1,249,908,038
Celgene (CELG): $1,146,230,554
Nvidia (NVDA): $1,141,786,517
iShares Nasdaq Biotechnology Fund (IBB): $1,122,655,652

Testing criteria:

1. Time interval used for the test: five years, ending December 1, 2016
2. Entry: on the close of the third consecutive down day
3. Filter: the instrument (stock or ETF) is trading above the twenty-day simple moving average
4. Exit: the trade is exited on the close of the third day after the entry

These are the aggregated results:

Trading Instrument	Av. Trade (%)	% Winners	Av. Win %/ Av. Loss %	# trades
Apple (AAPL)	0,76%	53%	1,71	31
Powershares Nasdaq 100 ETF (QQQ)	0,62%	68%	1,56	19
Amazon.com (AMZN)	2,24%	77%	2,14	35
Facebook (FB)	0,65%	65%	0,9	26
Microsoft (MSFT)	0,55%	66%	0,99	29
Alphabet (GOOG)	-0,11%	44%	1,12	25
Ishares 20+ Year Treasuries (TLT)	0,71%	73%	1,49	15
Celgene (CELG)	0,79%	70%	0,98	27
Nvidia (NVDA)	-0,46%	42%	0,9	33
Ishares Biotech Fund (IBB)	0,63%	60%	1,46	25
Average results	**0,64%**	**61,80%**	**1,33**	**26,50**

After this initial good overall set of results, I decided to test a slightly different exit. Instead of exiting on the close of the third day, I decided to test an exit on the close of the fifth day after the entry.

New Testing Criteria:

* Time interval used for the test: five years, ending December 1, 2016
* Entry: on the close of the third consecutive down day
* Filter: the instrument (stock or ETF) is trading above the twenty-day simple moving average
* Exit: the trade is exited on the close of the fifth day after the entry

These are the aggregated results:

Trading Instrument	Av. Trade (%)	% Winners	Av Win %/ Av. Loss %	# trades
Apple (AAPL)	0,50%	52%	1,39	31
Powershares Nasdaq 100 ETF (QQQ)	0,85%	68%	2,11	19
Amazon.com (AMZN)	2,81%	80%	3,27	35
Facebook (FB)	1,37%	69%	0,99	26
Microsoft (MSFT)	0,67%	59%	1,26	29
Alphabet (GOOG)	-0,07%	44%	1,39	25
Ishares 20+ Year Treasuries (TLT)	0,84%	67%	1,96	15
Celgene (CELG)	0,68%	67%	0,81	27
Nvidia (NVDA)	0,17%	53%	0,86	32
Ishares Biotech Fund (IBB)	0,61%	60%	1,37	25
Average results	**0,84%**	**61,90%**	**1,54**	**26,40**

The results are overall very satisfactory. The average winning trade is 0.64 percent for the three-day holding period and 0.84 percent for the five-day holding period, with winning rates of around 62 percent for both strategies.

Encouraged by the results, I decided to expand the testing sample, adding ten more trading instruments to the study. I added the ten most active (by dollar volume) tickers on the NYSE, on the same trading day, December 7.

Ten Most Active Tickers, NYSE:

Bank of America (BAC): $3,781,631,509
Wells Fargo (WFC): $2,669,700,397
Citigroup (C): $1,801,940,326
J. P. Morgan (JPM): $1,594,380,236
Goldman Sachs (GS): $1,552,399,526
Pfizer (PFE): $1,373,365,223
AT&T (T): $1,330,176,245
Allergan (AGN): $1,308,621,124
Johnson & Johnson (JNJ): $1,306,399,791
Disney (DIS): $1,249,939,363

I used the same testing criteria:

* Time interval used for the test: five years, ending December 1, 2016
* Entry: on the close of the third consecutive down day
* Filter: the instrument (stock or ETF) is trading above the twenty-day simple moving average
* Exit: the trade is exited on the close of the third day after the entry

These are the aggregated results for the ten NYSE tickers:

Trading Instrument	Av. Trade (%)	% Winners	Av. Win %/ Av. Loss %	# trades
Bank Of America (BAC)	0,64%	51%	1,77	35
Wells Fargo (WFC)	0,34%	58%	1,31	38
Citigroup (C)	1,10%	59%	2,26	37
J.P. Morgan (JPM)	0,82%	70%	2,27	30
Goldman Sachs (GS)	0,92%	58%	1,68	26
Pfizer (PFE)	-0,11%	49%	0,94	45
AT&T (T)	0,17%	53%	1,27	32
Allergan (AGN)	0,78%	64%	1,2	36
Johnson & Johnson (JNJ)	-0,15%	54%	0,51	24
Disney (DIS)	0,62%	65%	1,65	26
Average results	**0,51%**	**57,33%**	**1,47**	**33,67**

Again the results were very encouraging. I also tested the five-day holding period. These were the results:

Trading Instrument	Av. Trade (%)	% Winners	Av. Win %/ Av. Loss %	# trades
Bank Of America (BAC)	1,44%	63%	1,7	35
Wells Fargo (WFC)	0,79%	66%	1,5	38
Citigroup (C)	1,16%	62%	1,52	37
J.P. Morgan (JPM)	1,17%	73%	3,4	30
Goldman Sachs (GS)	2,24%	65%	2,27	26
Pfizer (PFE)	0,50%	62%	1,02	45
AT&T (T)	0,12%	56%	1	32
Allergan (AGN)	1,68%	69%	1,37	36
Johnson & Johnson (JNJ)	-0,03%	54%	0,86	24
Disney (DIS)	0,62%	81%	1,43	26
Average results	0,97%	63,33%	1,61	33,67

Again the results were solid. As in the first sample, the average gain improved with the five-day holding period. This looks like a very interesting base to develop a trading edge around this concept.

There are some considerations I would make about this study and this trading strategy.

First, where would I take this study next? I would start by expanding the sample, adding ten more midcap stocks and the sector ETFs. Another interesting step could be to test a four-day decline as the entry setup instead of the current three consecutive down days and test with different moving averages as filters.

Note that a strategy like this has a lot of opportunity, as there are always stocks that meet the criteria for opening a position. It also has positive expectancy, as the average gain per trade is large enough to cover commission costs and slippage. It meets the criteria set in chapter 2.

On the negative side, what I consider to be the weakest characteristic for this strategy is the lack of risk control on a trade-by-trade basis, as this strategy does not have stop-losses—though, of course, you can move this research in that direction and add stops to every individual position. One way to partially overcome that handicap is to open several trades at the same time, with a limit of, for example, 20 percent of the trading account on a single position. That would defend the account against a catastrophic adverse move on a single position.

I would expand this research project by adding an equity curve for the strategy to see its smoothness, analyze the drawdowns, and also check the month-by-month performance. One thing I highly value in trading systems is how constant the returns are—in other words, their consistency. If a strategy has, for example, four losing months on average per year, it is inferior to one that has only one losing month on average per year, even if the overall performance statistics for that particular system are less appealing. The reason for this is that you can depend on the strategy for income if the strategy is very reliable and shows consistency in its monthly returns.

Another thing I would add to this research would be testing in different five-year intervals (testing 2006 to 2011 and 2001 to 2006) and comparing the results.

If this strategy seems to fit your needs, try to keep developing it by adding your twists and finding ways to refine and adapt it to your trading needs or preferences.

Final thoughts on backtesting

When you backtest something, it allows you not only to test how a particular set of rules have worked in the past but also, even more importantly, to clarify your own approach so you can translate it into computer code. By doing as much, you'll be able to see if there is something that's not yet sufficiently clear in your thinking that you have not noticed.

(Disclaimer: This book is meant to be educational and should not be used as trading advice. All traders should gather information from multiple sources and create their own trading systems. The author makes no guarantees related to the claims contained herein. Please trade responsibly.)

Appendix C: Reinforcing the Message

have gathered some of the best market quotes about a few trading topics pertinent to this course. I've always found trading quotes to be an excellent source of trading wisdom—a lot of knowledge condensed in just a few words. My objective here is to reinforce the main messages of the book in areas I consider vital to successful trading. Because these areas are so important, they have been addressed also by some of the best traders of all time and by some of the brightest minds in the trading business now.

There are so many trading mistakes that I probably could not list them all, but some of the most common trading mistakes are averaging down, not respecting predefined stop-losses, overtrading, and placing the stops too close to the entry price. In my opinion, the biggest trading mistake of all is one that is not that evident at first sight: trading without a proven trading edge.

"Don't average losing trades. Be smaller than you need to be. Take profits."

—Larry Benedict, hedge-fund manager

"One of the most suicidal things you can do in trading is to keep adding to a losing position."

—Marty Schwartz, S&P futures trader

"Never, ever change a stop-loss."

—Andrew Keene, options trader

"Placing stops too close will likely lead to multiple losses. Will lead traders to want to get back in because they do not think they were wrong."

—Colm O'Shea, hedge-fund manager

"Every experienced stock trader knows overtrading is his greatest weakness, but he continues to allow this weakness to be his ruin."

—W. D. Gann, market technician

"I see that a significant number of my poor trades were triggered by my desire to do something."

—Rick Williams, professional trader

"Not predefining your risk, not cutting your losses, or not systematically taking profits are three of the most common—and usually the most costly—trading errors that you can make."

—Mark Douglas, trading author

"We are in the business of making mistakes. Winners make small mistakes, losers make big mistakes."

—Ned Davis, market strategist

"If you have made a mistake, deal with the mistake, don't compound it."

—Michael Steinhardt, hedge-fund manager

"If you do not have a competitive advantage, do not compete."
—Jack Welch, business executive

Another crucial area is trading experience. In the book Outliers, author Malcolm Gladwell notes that it takes roughly ten thousand hours of practice to achieve mastery in a given field. Well, I do not know the exact number of hours needed to master trading, but I know that in trading, experience is irreplaceable—if you are able to add experience to knowledge, you will obtain trading wisdom.

"Gaining proficiency is the same in trading as in any other profession—it requires experience, and experience takes time."
—Mark D. Cook, S&P Futures trader

"The two most difficult things at the stock market are to accept a loss and not realize a small profit."
—Andre Kostolany, speculator

"There is no substitute for the improvement power of screen time."
—Mike Bellafiore, prop trader

"Amateur traders lose money because they try to avoid losing. Professional traders understand they need to take losses to win."
—Jack Schwager, trading author

"We all know when we are wrong. The market will tell the speculator when he is wrong, because he is losing money."
—Jesse Livermore, speculator

"Learning solely from actual experience, however, is inadequate because it takes too much time to get a representative sample to determine whether a decision rule works."
—Ray Dalio, hedge-fund manager

Professional traders and athletes develop good practices as they perfect their craft. I have gathered a few quotes on best practices, including one from a basketball coach. There are interesting similarities between how to achieve a very high level of performance in sports and in trading. One is the ability to review our performance and make small improvements daily.

"The best trading book you can ever read is your own trading journal."

—Anonymous trader

"Excellence is the gradual result of always striving to do better."
—Pat Riley, basketball coach

"Nothing like a closed market to see the charts clearly. Use this quiet time to review without bias or emotions."
—Dan Zanger, momentum stocks trader

"I focus on three things: price, moving averages, and one momentum oscillator. That's it. My trading process takes less than fifteen minutes a day, and most days I do nothing."
—Larry Tentarelli, intermediate-term technical trader

"There are some things that winners do that losing traders often ignore. Keeping a trading journal, of some kind, is one of those practices."
—Adam Grimes, systematic trader

Trading is a mind game. One of the characteristics of top traders is that they know themselves and are able to play their strengths in the markets. Also, traders must also learn to accept and embrace small losses and overcome the resistance to pull the trigger on cutting a losing trade before it causes any real damage to the trader's account.

"What character traits define world-class traders? Answer: Self-Awareness, they know themselves, their strong points and weaknesses."
—Peter Brandt, technical trader

"If you are shocked or shaken by small losses, you're probably not ready to be a trader. This is part of the game and your edge in the markets."
—Dan Zanger, momentum stocks trader

"Most studies suggest that losses are twice as powerful, psychologically, as gains."
—Daniel Kahneman, psychologist

Markets are mostly random, as most trading edges are very difficult to find. Also, if you are trading without a plan, you are basically playing the randomness of the markets, unable to make much progress.

"To my way of thinking, randomness is the enemy—if something is random, we can't make money with it."
—Adam Grimes, systematic trader

"Too many new traders have no signals, no system, and no plan. They rely on the randomness of their own opinions and predictions. There is no edge."
—Steve Burns, indexes swing trader

"Focus on whether what you are doing is right, not on the random nature of any single trade's outcome."
—Richard Dennis, commodities trader

I addressed the topic of changing market conditions in the course. Traders who are able to see change and adapt have the best chances of lasting success trading the markets. Kyosaki says it best: change will happen whether you embrace it or not.

"You adapt, evolve, compete, or die."
—Paul Tudor Jones, hedge-fund manager

"In trading, we cannot direct the wind, but we can adjust our sails. And that's all you need to know and do."
—Mark Minervini, momentum stocks trader

"Quite often the biggest drawdown happens when the market type changes."
—Van Tharp, trading coach

"If there's one lesson to learn about any industry or economy, it's that change must be embraced. Change will happen whether you do or not."
—Robert Kyosaki, investor

Ignoring market noise is as difficult as controlling overtrading or flawlessly executing a business plan. Your edge will be fully functional only if you are able to ignore what is not relevant to your strategy. One thing that helps some traders focus more on what really matters and ignore market noise is to turn the off financial TV (e.g., CNBC and Bloomberg) and Twitter during trading hours.

"Most days, eighty to ninety percent of what you hear, read or see about the market is worthless noise."
—Ed Borgato, investor

"Everything I need to know is based on a stock's price behavior and volume; the rest is pure noise."
—Dan Zanger, momentum stocks trader

"The hallmark of a pro trader is to operate within your own circle of competence and ignore everything else."
—Mark Minervini, momentum stocks trader

Successful traders are original thinkers; they do not follow conventional wisdom. You must be able to be creative and use market data in new ways or see new relationships in the data.

"Whether in starting a business or investing in financial markets, outstanding results spring from original thinking and original ideas. The key to novel, creative thinking is observation."
—Brett Steenbarger, trading coach

"Make little observations about what the market is doing; you'll come up with lots of ideas."
—Rob Hanna, trading expert

"Successful traders look at markets in unique ways."
—Brett Steenbarger, trading coach

"Successful traders isolate themselves from the opinion of others."
—Linda Raschke, professional trader

When traders have a winning trade on, they always feel they have too little size on; when the trade is losing, the trade size always seems too big and inappropriate. Traders must learn the right level of risk to take at any given time.

"If your positions are getting you emotional or keeping you up at night, you are trading too large. Position down to the sleeping point."
—Mark Minervini, momentum stocks trader

"Traders focus almost entirely on where to enter a trade. In reality, the entry size is often more important than the entry price because if the size is too large, a trader will be more likely to exit a good trade on a meaningless adverse price move."

—Steve Clark, hedge-fund manager

"I would say that risk management is the most important thing to be well understood. Undertrade, undertrade, undertrade is my second piece of advice. Whatever you think your position ought to be, cut it at least in half."

—Bruce Kovner, hedge-fund manager

When choosing a trading system, it's always better to go for a robust methodology than to come up with something that looks very good on paper because it was overoptimized and has no adherence to future prices because it was fine-tuned to work only with a set of past data.

"In trading, robust is often a lot better than elegant and precise."

—Mark D. Cook, S&P futures trader

"Most people do far more fitting than they need to or should do."

—Robert Carver, systematic trader

If you want to cultivate strength in your trading, go for consistency. Learn to do the same trades over and over again. Believing in your own consistency may even be the most important component in your ability to keep extracting money from the market over a long period of time, according to Mark Douglas.

"The most important component in a trader's ability to accumulate money over time is having a belief in his own consistency."

—Mark Douglas, trading author

"The superior traders gravitate to a single approach—the specific approach is not important—and become extremely adept at it."
— Charles Faulkner, NLP practitioner

"If you really want to make this a business, grind it out, do the same thing every day."
— Thomas Striedman, trading-systems expert

"A good example of a bad thing is a trader who randomly pulls up different indicators when considering a trade. There's no way to know what indicators he will use or how he will interpret them, so this trader is just throwing darts."
— Adam Grimes, systematic trader

No trader will be able to enjoy success in the market if he does not have the patience to wait for the trading signal to enter a position and the patience to calmly wait for the signal to close it out. This is a rare skill among novice traders.

"Doing nothing requires the patience of a saint. It is common for traders who develop good methodologies that signal trades infrequently to take other trades that lack the appropriate criteria because of a need to do something."
— Jack Schwager, trading author

"The stock market rewards patience with winning stocks and punishes patience when you hold on to losing stocks."
— Steve Burns, swing trader

"One down day doesn't mean your system is broken."
— Robert Carver, systematic trader

"Being bored while trading and having the discipline to do nothing is a skill."

—Steve Burns, swing trader

"When you get to a point where you are patient and only take quality trades, you have decided you are not in it for action but to make money."

—Mark Minervini, momentum stocks trader

Most traders will benefit from avoiding trading in very volatile markets, but the irony is that traders are attracted to volatile markets because those are the ones that get most media coverage.

"Volatility is like a naked flame. It attracts traders like moths and then burns them."

—Assad Tannous, professional money manager

Try to keep your trading as simple as possible. You don't need many instruments, trading screens, technical indicators, or parameters in your trading system. In trading, less is more.

"The most robust system has the fewest parameters."

—Perry Kaufman, trading-systems expert

"A high-level technical trader needs only a chart and a quiet room."

—Larry Tentarelli, intermediate-term technical trader

"Very often the simplest thing you can come up with works the best."

—Tomas Nesnidal, independent futures trader

"Everything I need to know is based on a stock's price behavior and volume. The rest is pure noise."

—Dan Zanger, momentum stocks trader

Successful traders are confident in their abilities to win over the long term. Confidence comes both from good past experiences of winning but also from solid preparation that comes from good market research.

"As a psychologist, I am impressed by the degree to which traders who prepare rigorously feel as though they deserve to win."
—Brett Steenbarger, trading coach

"If you have to ask someone what they think about a market then you don't have system."
—Dave Stendahl, systematic futures trader

"Confidence is every part of trading. If you are not convinced that you can win, you should never climb into the ring."
—Marty Schwartz, S&P futures trader

A trader must believe it's possible to consistently win trading the markets. They just need to work very hard in find a trading edge that is adequate for the size of his account, for his personality, and for his availability.

"There is no reason why a small trader can't find a niche and pull some money out of it."
—Michael Himmel, artificial-intelligence expert

"I believe there is a direct correlation between the amount of preparation one does as a trader and the bottom line results obtained."
—Tom Basso, hedge-fund manager

"Only one who devotes himself to a cause with his whole strength and soul can be a true master. For this reason mastery demands all of a person."
—Albert Einstein, physicist

"Strong motivation is a common characteristic among those who excel in any field."

—Charles Faulkner, NLP practitioner

"Wealth is the product of a man's capacity to think."

—Ayn Rand, philosopher

Appendix D: Glossary

Backtest. The process of testing a trading strategy over a period of time using historical data.

Bear market. A market characterized by declining prices.

Breakout. A price that is moving beyond a previous high or low, moving outside the boundaries of a previous price range.

Bollinger bands. A technical indicator developed by John Bollinger, a Bollinger band is plotted two standard deviations away from a simple moving average, but traders can customize the value in most charting platforms.

Bull market. A market characterized by rising prices.

Chart. A graph that depicts the price movement of a stock or market. Most common charts are daily bar charts that highlight the open, high, low, and close for each trading session.

Commodities. Physical products traded at futures exchanges such as crude oil, gold, or grains.

Contract. A single unit of a commodity or future. Futures contracts are standardized traded instruments of commodities or financial assets traded in futures exchanges.

Contrarian. A trader or investor who trades against the majority of traders.

Day trade. A trade that is initiated and closed on the same day.

Day trader. A trader who specializes in opening and closing trading positions in the same day.

Discretionary trader. A trader who makes decisions based on his interpretation of the market, based on instincts, rather than acting on signals generated by a mechanical trading system.

Diversification. Investing in different stocks or markets to reduce overall risk.

Down trend. A general tendency for declining prices in a given stock or market.

Drawdown. A drawdown is the peak-to-trough decline during a specific period suffered by a trading account. A drawdown is normally expressed as the percentage between the peak and the subsequent trough.

Edge. A trading edge is a technique or approach that creates an advantage over other market players.

Entry signal. The part of your trading system that signals when you should be initiating a new trade.

Equity curve. The graphical representation of the change in value of a trading account over time.

Exit signal. The part of your system that tells you when to close an open trading position.

Expectancy. How much a trader can expect to make on average over many trades.

Forex. Foreign-exchange markets, the market of foreign currencies.

Gap. The space between prices on a chart that occurs when the price of an asset makes a sharp move up or down with no trading occurring in the prices between the last closing price and the new opening price.

Indicator. In the context of technical analysis, an indicator is a mathematical calculation based on a stock's price, such as the Relative Strength Index (RSI) or a moving average.

Leverage. The use of various financial instruments (futures or options) or borrowed capital to increase the potential return of an investment or trade.

Long. A trading position that is initiated with a buy order and that profits from a rising price market.

Market prediction. A guess about the future direction of prices.

Mechanical trading. A trading style where all buy and sell actions are determined by a computer.

Momentum. The force or speed of a price movement. It can be measured in percentage terms using the Rate of Change (ROC) technical indicator.

Moving average. A widely used technical-analysis indicator that smooths the price action. The most commonly used is the simple average of a stock or market over a defined number of time periods. The most common application of moving averages is to identify the trend direction.

Overbought. A term used in technical analysis to describe a situation where a stock or a market has risen to such a degree that an oscillator reaches its upper bounds.

Oversold. A term used in technical analysis to describe a situation where a stock or a market has fallen to such a degree that an oscillator reaches its lower bounds.

P&L. The sum of your profits and losses for a given period of time.

Position sizing. How large a position you put on a particular trade. An algorithm can be used to determine the position sizing according to your equity.

Positive Expectancy. A trading system that will make money over the long term. A system where the average trade is profitable.

Profit factor. The profit factor is calculated by dividing the total sum of your winning trades by the total sum of your losing trades. The higher the ratio, the better the trading strategy or the trader.

Random. A number that cannot be predicted. Determined by chance.

Relative strength. A measure of a stock's price strength relative to the general stock market.

Resistance. A resistance level is a price above the market where the security could not overcome in the past and retraced.

Range day. A day where the price has no meaningful direction over the course of the day, trading back and forth.

Seasonality. Trading based on predictable changes in price during certain times of the month or year.

Setup. You have a trading setup when certain criteria are present before you enter a trade.

Short position. A bet on declining prices by selling an asset you do not own in order to buy it back in the future at a lower price and book the profit. When you sell before buying, you are shorting the market.

Slippage. The difference between the theoretical execution price on a trade and the actual fill price.

Stop-loss order. A sell order placed below the market that becomes a market order when the specified price is reached. It is an order used to limit losses.

Support. A support level is a price below the current price where a stock or a market has bounced in the past or has had difficulty falling through it.

Swing trader. A trader who holds positions in the market for several days or weeks.

Tick. The minimum fluctuation of a stock, ETF, or futures contract.

Trading edge. A trading edge is present when you can anticipate the evolution of the market for a specific period after specified market conditions have been met.

Trading System. A trading system is a set of organized thoughts set out in a logical trading plan that tells you when to buy, sell, or exit and how much to risk in every trade you take.

Trending day. A trading session where prices trade in one direction, either up or down, from the open to the close.

Systematic trader. A trader who buys and sells according to the signals generated by a trading system.

Trend. The tendency for prices to move in a given direction, up or down.

Trend-following system. A trading system that generates buy and sell signals in the direction of the market's trend.

Volatility. A statistical measure of the price variability of a stock or market index. A volatile market is subject to wide price fluctuations. The higher the volatility, the riskier the stock.

Volume. Total number of shares or contracts traded in a given day.

www.ingramcontent.com/pod-product-compliance
Lightning Source LLC
Chambersburg PA
CBHW070029210526
45170CB00012B/502